the essenti[al]

Musée d'Orsay

...and our favorites...

* The numbers indicate the sections.

The Marais

© Bertrand Gardel / hemis.fr

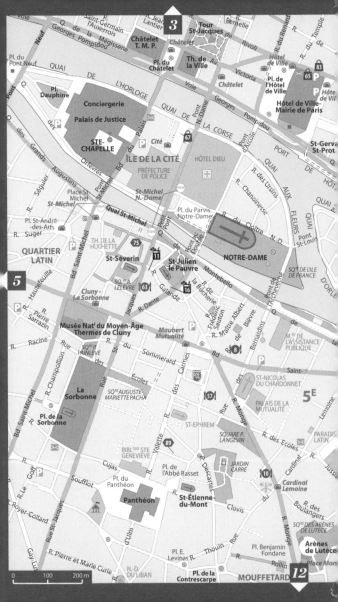

VOIE
Q. de la Mégisserie
Georges Pompidou
Saint-Germain l'Auxerrois
R. Jean Lantier
Tour St-Jacques
R. de la Verrerie
R. du Renard
R. du Temple

Pl. du Pont Neuf
QUAI DE L'HORLOGE
Châtelet
T. M. P.
Châtelet
Th. de la Ville
Av.
Victoria
Hôtel de Ville
65
83
P
P
Hôtel de Vil

Pl. Dauphine
Conciergerie
Palais de Justice
STE-CHAPELLE
Cité
P
ÎLE DE LA CITÉ
PRÉFECTURE DE POLICE
Pl. du Châtelet
Voie
Georges Pompidou
N.-DAME
LA CORSE
HÔTEL DIEU
67
Châtelet
Pl. de l'Hôtel de Ville
Hôtel de Ville-Mairie de Paris
St-Gerva St-Prot
QUAI DE HÔT
PONT
AUX FLEURS
QUAI
Pont St-Louis

des Grands Augustins
Séguier
Orfèvres
St-Michel
R. des Ursins
R. Chanoinesse
QUAI
Pont St-Louis

Place St-André-des-Arts
Suger
St-Michel
Pl. St-André-des-Arts
Quai St-Michel
St-Michel N.-Dame
Pl. du Parvis Notre-Dame
R. du Cloître N.-D.
NOTRE-DAME
SQ DE L'ÎLE DE FRANCE
SQ DE L'ÎLE DE FRANCE
PONT ST-LOUIS
QUAI D'ORLE

QUARTIER LATIN
Haurefeuille
TH. DE LA HUCHETTE
75
St-Séverin
11
St-Julien le Pauvre
Montebello
R. de la Bûcherie
R. Frédéric Sauton
R. Maître Albert
de Bièvre
des Bernardins
M.on DE L'ASSISTANCE PUBLIQUE

5
R. Pierre Sarrazin
Cluny-La Sorbonne
63
Galande
16
R. Dante
R. Lagrange
P
8
Saint-

Musée Nat' du Moyen-Âge
Thermes de Cluny
Maubert Mutualité
Bd
St-Germain
ST-NICOLAS DU CHARDONNET

R. Racine
R. Champollion
SQ P. PAINLEVÉ
R. du Sommerard
des
Carmes
POL
Rue Monge
PALAIS DE LA MUTUALITÉ
5E
Lemoine

La Sorbonne
SQ AUGUSTE MARIETTE PACHA
Écoles
57
ST-EPHREM
SQUARE P. LANGEVIN
R. des Écoles
PARADIS LATIN
Jussie

Pl. de la Sorbonne
Bd Saint-Michel
BIBL QUE STE GENEVIÈVE
Valette
89
R. des
10
Cardinal Lemoine
R. des Boulangers
Monge

Le Goff
Soufflot
Cujas
Pl. du Panthéon
Pl. de l'Abbé Basset
JARDIN CARRÉ
Cardinal Lemoine
SQ DES ARÈNES DE LUTÈCE

R. Royer-Collard
Panthéon
St-Étienne-du-Mont
Descartes
Clovis
Arènes de Lutèce
Place Mon

R. Pierre et Marie Curie
Gay-Lus
d'Ulm
N.-D. DU LIBAN
Pl. E. Levinas R.
Thouin
Rue
Pl. Benjamin Fondane
Rollin
12

Pl. de la Contrescarpe
MOUFFETARD

0   100   200 m

WHERE TO EAT

🔟 Aux Verres de Contact – *33 r. de Bièvre* - ⓜ *Maubert-Mutualité* - 🕿 *01 46 34 58 02* - *www.auxverresdecontact.com* - *closed Sat lunch and Sun* - *main courses €29-35.* A convivial, modern bistrot serving good value dishes.

🔟 Strada Café – *24 r. du Monger* - ⓜ *Cardinal-Lemoine* - 🕿 *09 72 45 12 87* - *www.stradacafe.fr* - *open mornings until 18h30m* - *set menus €7.50/15.* A cozy café that serves excellent lunch options, as well as pastries, fresh fruit juice, and organic coffee, all in a cheerful environment.

🔟 Lhassa – *13 r. de la Montagne-Ste-Geneviève* - ⓜ *Maubert-Mutualité* - 🕿 *01 43 26 22 19* - *price range €15-30.* A price-wise Tibetan restaurant offering house-made yogurt, sautéed marinated beef and grilled dumplings.

🔟 Les Fous de l'Île – *33 r. des Deux-Ponts* - ⓜ *Pont-Marie* - 🕿 *01 43 25 76 67* - *www.lesfousdelile.com* - *main courses €18.* Good humour reigns in this néo-bistrot on the île Saint-Louis, where traditional French fare goes modern.

🔟 Mirama – *17 r. St-Jacques* - ⓜ *Cluny-la-Sorbonne* - 🕿 *01 43 54 71 77* - *main courses €10-14.* Connoisseurs of authentic Chinese cuisine flock to this restaurant tucked behind Saint-Séverin church.

TAKE A BREAK

🔟 Berthillon – *29 et 31 r. St-Louis-en-l'Île* - ⓜ *Pont-Marie* - *closed Mon-Tue.* This is the most famous ice-cream parlour in Paris, and the tea room is cosy to boot.

🔟 Odette – *77 r. Galande* - ⓜ *Cluny-la-Sorbonne.* Excellent place to try cream puffs in the small retro room upstairs.

🔟 La Fourmi Ailée – *8 r. du Fouarre* - ⓜ *Maubert-Mutualité.* A charming tea

Berthillon

room-restaurant in a former book-store, serving pastries, salads, daily specials and a wide choice of teas.

SHOPPING

Bouquinistes – *Quai St-Michel.* On the banks of the Seine, the booksellers install their green crates packed with old books, engravings, drawings and magazines.

🔟 Marché aux Fleurs – *Pl. Louis-Lépine* - ⓜ *Cité - closed Mon.* Created in 1808, this flower market forms a bucolic enclave on the île de la Cité. On Sundays, birds replace flowers.

NIGHTLIFE

🔟 Caveau de la Huchette – *5 r. de la Huchette* - ⓜ *St-Michel - closed Sun.* A temple of jazz in central Paris, in a vaulted cellar in the Latin Quartier.

🔟 Le Piano Vache – *8 r. Laplace* - ⓜ *Maubert-Mutualité - closed Sun.* A hot spot for local students, where a coffee still costs just €1. In the evenings, enjoy rock, 80s music or Gypsy jazz.

🔟 The Pledge – *19 r. des Deux-Ponts* - ⓜ *Pont-Marie.* A pleasant bar on the île Saint-Louis. Enjoy a drink and nibbles, and dance all night long.

Entries appear in the neighboring quartier:

🔟 ▶ 3

🔟 🔟 🔟 🔟 🔟 🔟 🔟 ▶ 4

This is the historic cradle of Paris. Île de la Cité, home to Notre-Dame, remains one of the most attractive districts in the city. The Quartier Latin, on the other side of the Seine, retains an old-world charm, with its student life, art-house cinemas and ancient ruins.

VISIT

Cathédrale Notre-Dame

Cathédrale Notre-Dame★★★ - 🚇 Cité, RER B St-Michel-Notre-Dame. People have been praying at this spot for 20 centuries, yet the first stone of the most famous church in Paris wasn't laid before 1163. From the top of the south tower (*10h-18h30, winter 17:30, late night in summer - €8.50*), there is a splendid view of the spire, the flying buttresses and la Cité.

Palais de Justice★ - *10 bd du Palais* - 🚇 Cité - *8h30-18h - closed weekends*. The heavily remodeled former palace of the kings of France was assigned to Parliament, and later to Justice. The Salle des Pas Perdus was formerly the *grand'salle* of Philippe le Bel.

Sainte-Chapelle★★★ - *8 bd du Palais* - 🚇 Cité - *www.sainte-chapelle.fr - 9h30-18h (winter 9h-17h) - €10*. A Gothic chapel built in 13C by Saint Louis to house the Passion relics, its stained-glass windows are the oldest in Paris.

Conciergerie★★ - 🚇 Cité - *www. paris-conciergerie.fr - 9h30-18h - (Wed 20h) - €9 (€15 in combo w/Sainte-Chapelle)..* This vestige of the Cité's palace, where the kings of France lived, was once a prison. Thousands of condemned were held here, amongst them Marie-Antoinette and Danton.

Pont Neuf★ - 🚇 Pont-Neuf. Built in 1604, this is the oldest bridge in Paris.

Île Saint-Louis★★ - 🚇 Cité, Pont-Marie. This charming island has a village-like feel with its 17C mansions and magnificent views of Notre-Dame.

Institut du Monde arabe★ - *1 r. des Fossés-St-Bernard* - 🚇 Jussieu, Cardinal-Lemoine - *www.imarabe.org - 10h-18h (Sat-Sun 19h) - €8*. Created to promote a better understanding of Arab civilisation, this Jean Nouvel-designed building houses a museum, library, cinema, restaurant and peaceful café.

Panthéon★★ - *RER B Luxembourg - 10h-18h30 Oct-Mar 18h) - €9*. The tombs of more than 70 French personalities, from Voltaire to Jean Moulin, lie underneath this majestic (18C) dome.

Église Saint-Étienne-du-Mont★ - *1 pl. Ste-Geneviève - RER B Luxembourg*. Admire the 16C sculpted rood screen, and its organ, the oldest in Paris.

La Sorbonne★ - 🚇 Cluny-la-Sorbonne. This illustrious university, founded in 13C, has an international reputation and a beautiful 17C Jesuit-style church.

Musée national du Moyen Âge - Thermes de Cluny★★ - *6 pl. Paul-Painlevé* - 🚇 Cluny-la-Sorbonne - *www.musee-moyenage.fr - 9h15-17h45 - closed Tue - €9*. The ancient mansion of the abbots of Cluny (15C), adjoining the 3C Roman baths, houses a museum devoted to the Middle Ages. The highlight of the exhibits is the Dame à la Licorne tapestries.

Église Saint-Séverin★★ - 🚇 Cluny-la-Sorbonne. The central *palmier* pillar in the flamboyant Gothic choir, the multi-coloured stained-glass windows by Jean Bazaine (20C) and a small cloister are all noteworthy.

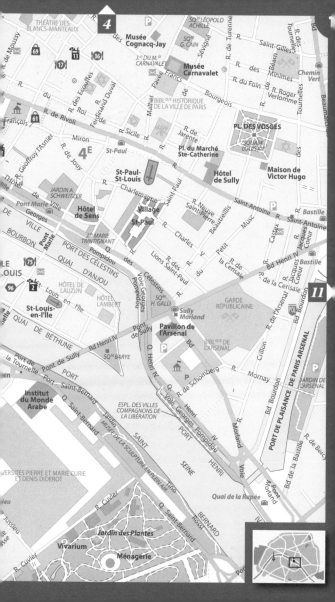

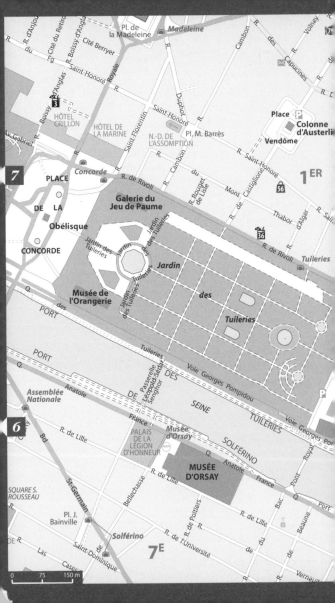

The more stylish and flavourful **Café Richelieu Angelina** 🍴 on the 1st floor of the Richelieu wing, has a splendid view of the Pyramide (*01 49 27 93 31 - www.angelina-paris.fr - closed evenings and Tue - main courses €16-28*).

🍴9 Baan Boran – *3 r. Montpensier - ⓜ Palais-Royal-Musée-de-Louvre - 01 40 15 90 45 - www.baan-boran.fr - closed Sat lunch and Sun - main courses €15-20.* Enjoy Thai dishes in this refined restaurant, facing the Palais-Royal theatre.

🍴26 Gwadar – *39 r. St-Roch - ⓜ Pyramides - 01 42 96 28 24 - closed Sun - main courses €10-20.* This is a relaxing, cosy Pakistani restaurant, with friendly service.

🍴60 Le Stube – *31 r. de Richelieu - ⓜ Palais-Royal - 01 45 08 03 59 - www.louvrebouteille.fr - closed Sun, Mon - main courses €5-10.* German snacks salty and sweet. On the menu: savoury pies, sandwiches, currywurst, sauerkraut, Black Forest cake, strudel, and more.

🍴64 Nodaiwa – *272 r. St-Honoré - ⓜ Palais-Royal-Musée-de-Louvre - 01 42 86 03 42 - www.nodaiwa.com - closed Sun - menus start at 20 €.* Grilled eel is the restaurant's speciality.

🍴80 Zen – *8 r. de l'Échelle - ⓜ Palais-Royal-Musée-de-Louvre - 01 42 61 93 99 - closed Mon - main courses 10-20 €.* Authentic cuisine is served in this Japanese canteen.

TAKE A BREAK

🍵36 Angelina – *226 r. de Rivoli - ⓜ Tuileries.* A beautiful tradititional tea room, famous for its pastries and creamy hot chocolate.

🍵5 Café Marly – *Musée du Louvre - ⓜ Tuileries.* Situated in the Richelieu wing of Musée du Louvre, this is the ideal spot to sip tea and contemplate the Pyramide of Pei.

Angelina

🍵24 Le Fumoir – *6 r. de l'Amiral-de-Coligny - ⓜ Louvre-Rivoli.* An intimate, clubby place with leather armchairsand bench seats. There is a café, tea room, restaurant, and library.

SHOPPING

🛍 In addition to the Louvre's great bookshop, the **Carrousel du Louvre** 🛍78 (*99 r. de Rivoli - ⓜ Palais-Royal-Musée-de-Louvre*) offers fashion boutiques, jewellery, home decoration, gifts etc. The **Palais-Royal arcades** 🛍79 (*ⓜ Palais-Royal-Musée-de-Louvre*) offer great, if pricey, window-shopping. Likewise for the **Véro-Dodat arcade** 🛍77 (*ⓜ Louvre-Rivoli*). Continue shopping along the **rue des Petits-Champs** (*ⓜ Louvre-Rivoli*) and in the Vivienne arcade (🛍 *Quartier 8*).

NIGHTLIFE

🌙95 Au Caveau Montpensier – *15 r. de Montpensier - ⓜ Palais-Royal-Musée-de-Louvre - from 17h30 - closed Sun* A discreet, cosy bar popular with expats. Billiards in one of the vaulted rooms.

Entries appear in the neighboring quartier:
🏛12 ▶ 3
🏛11 ▶ 7
🍴13 🍴25 🍴70 🎭29 🛍77 ▶ 8

This quartier is packed with prestigious museums, from Musée d'Orsay with its Impressionist masterpieces to the Palais du Louvre, which houses one of the largest art collections in the world.

Musée du Louvre

VISIT

Musée du Louvre★★★ – *Palais-Royal-Musée-du-Louvre - www.louvre.fr - 9h-18h (Wed and Fri. 21h45) - closed Tue - €15.* This former royal palace has become a temple of art, with exhibits from antiquity to the middle of the 19C. The main entrance is behind I. M. Pei's transparent **Pyramid**. The museum has countless masterpieces: Léonard de Vinci's *Mona Lisa, The Raft of the Medusa* by Géricault and the *Vénus de Milo* are just a few of the highlights.

Palais Royal★★ – *Palais-Royal-Musée-du-Louvre.* The palace is home to the Constitutional Council, the Ministry of Culture and the Council of State. It is surrounded by 18C arcades, and the inner courtyard and garden provide the setting for the black and white columns of Daniel Buren (*Les Deux Plateaux,* 1986).

Place des Victoires★ – *Bourse.* This elegant square with symmetrical architecture was conceived by Marshal La Feuillade, in honour of Louis XIV, and designed by Jules Hardouin-Mansart.

Musée des Arts Décoratifs★★ – *107 r. de Rivoli - Palais-Royal-Musée-du-Louvre - www.lesartsdecoratifs.fr - 11h-18h (Thu 21h) - closed Mon - €11.* The collection of 5,000 objects showcases decorative arts from the Middle Ages to 21C: ceramics, furniture, gold work and silverware, jewellery, glassware, wallpaper, drawings and games. In the same building there are the **Musée de la Mode et du Textile** and the **Musée de la Publicité**.

Jardin des Tuileries★ – *Concorde, Tuileries.* This gorgeous park, which was created for Catherine de Médici and redesigned in 17C by Le Nôtre, is laid out with fountains, flower gardens, ponds and sculptures dating from the 17C to the present.

Galeries Nationales du Jeu de Paume – *Jardin des Tuileries - Concorde - www.jeudepaume.org - 11h-19h (Tue 21h) - closed Mon - €10.* An arts centre where the history of image can be traced through photography, video and multi-media supports.

Musée de l'Orangerie★★ – *Jardin des Tuileries - Concorde - www. musee-orangerie.fr - 9h-18h - closed Tue - €9.* The Orangerie is the perfect backdrop for the famous *Les Nymphéas* series by Claude Monet. The exhibition also includes works from the Walter-Guillaume collection (late 19C-early 20C).

Musée d'Orsay★★★ – *RER C Musée-d'Orsay - www.musee-orsay.fr - 9h30-18h (Thu 21h45) - closed Mon - €12.* The ancient Orsay train station houses one of the most famous museums in Paris. Its collection covers the period from 1848 to 1914. The Impressionist works are outstanding.

WHERE TO EAT

At the Louvre, a practical lunch option is the self-service **Restaurants du Monde**, *(11h30-20h30 - closed Tue eve - main courses €10-15).*

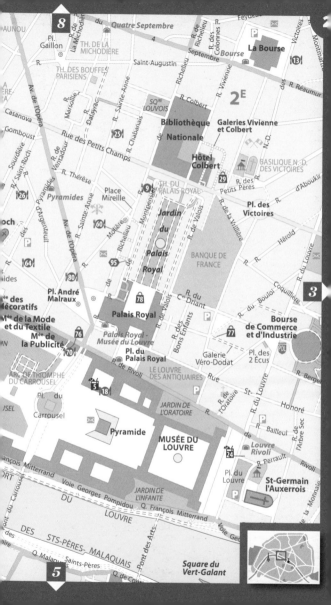

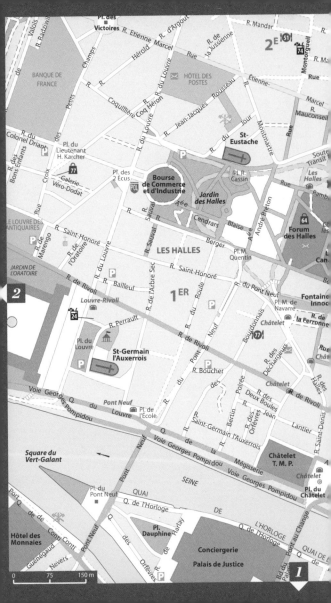

Kitchen – *74 r. des Gravilliers -* Arts-et-Métiers *- 09 52 55 11 66 - www.bobsjuicebar.com - closed evenings - main courses €6-9*. California-style organic and vegetarian choices (fresh juices, soups, salads, sandwiches) are served at communal tables.

La Marée Jeanne – *3 r. Mandar -* Sentier *- 01 42 61 58 34 - www.lamareejeanne.com - main courses €19-26*. A fashionable address where fish and shellfish, served as tapas or main dishes, are the order of the day.

Le Quincampe – *78 r. Quincampoix -* Rambuteau *- 01 40 27 01 45 - www.lequincampe.fr - closed Sat lunch and Sun evening - main courses €14-20*. A cosy, intimate restaurant, with a crackling open fireplace in winter. There are some Maghreb-inspired dishes.

Pirouette – *5 r. Montdétour -* Châtelet-Les Halles *- 01 40 26 47 81 - www.restaurantpirouette.com - closed Sun - fixed price menus €18 (lunch), €40-60 (dinner)*. A menu that plays on the classics. The dining room has chic Nordic décor.

Saudade – *34 r. des Bourdonnais -* Pont-Neuf *- 01 42 33 03 65 - www.restaurantsaudade.com - closed Sun and Aug - main courses €18-24*. For a taste of Portugal in the midst of Paris, meet at this intricately-tiled restaurant.

TAKE A BREAK

Le Georges – *Centre Pompidou -* Rambuteau *- closed Tue*. On the sixth floor of the Centre Pompidou, this minimalist, industrial-styled café-restaurant boasts an exceptional view of Paris.

Queen Ann – *5 r. Simon-le-Franc -* Rambuteau *- closed morings and Mon*. Expect to find home-made cakes, teas, steamy hot chocolate, savory tarts, and brunch on Sundays.

Pirouette

Stohrer – *51 r. Montorgueil -* Sentier. Classified as Monument Historique, this is the most beautiful store in the street. A mandatory stop for baba au rhum fans!

SHOPPING

The **rue Étienne-Marcel** and **rue Montorgueil** (Étienne-Marcel) are lined with trendy upscale stores. High street chains abound at the **Forum des Halles** or on the **rue de Rivoli**.

Bazar de l'Hôtel-de-Ville (BHV) – Hôtel-de-Ville *- closed Sun*. A hotch-potch of goods for sale in this Parisian temple; from clothes to tools.

Boutique de Paris – *29 r. de Rivoli -* Hôtel-de-Ville *- closed Sun*. The City of Light is available here in all forms: mugs, tea towels, carafes, chocolates, and so on.

NIGHTLIFE

Le Baiser Salé – *58 r. des Lombards -* Châtelet *- www.lebaisersale.com*. Jazz and world-fusion music.

Le Duc des Lombards – *42 r. des Lombards -* Châtelet *- www.ducdeslombards.com*. This is a famous jazz club and restaurant.

Entries appear in the neighboring quartier:

60 24 ▶ 2

62 69 79 74 ▶ 4

Since the 60s Les Halles, dubbed the *belly of Paris*, has been the stepping stone linking the capital to its suburbs. The redevelopment of the Forum aims to heal the image of this gateway to the riches of the Centre Pompidou.

VISIT

Forum and Les Halles garden – ⓜ *Châtelet-Les Halles.* Built in the 70s on the site of Les Halles food market and recently renovated, the Forum shopping mall is now covered with 18,000 glass scales that form an amazing canopy. The garden leads from the Forum to the district's ancient monuments, notably the circular structure of the **Bourse de Commerce** (18C-19C).

Église Saint-Eustache★★ – ⓜ *Châtelet-Les Halles.* Modelled on the plan of Notre-Dame in 16C, the church wasn't completed until 1754. The Renaissance style north façade has turrets capped with cupolas.

Quartier des Halles★ – ⓜ *Les Halles.* Les Halles, *the belly of Paris*, was a food market. Founded in 1135, merchants and craftsmen sold their wares twice a week. Neighboring roads are lined with shops and cafés, such as the **rue des Lombards**, a small medieval street, or the **rue de la Ferronrie**, where Henri IV was assinated by Ravaillac on 14th May 1610.

Rue Montorgueil – ⓜ *Étienne-Marcel.* Lined with cafes, restaurants and shops, this lively pedestrian street still has ancient houses (15, 17, 23, 25).

Rue Saint-Denis – ⓜ *Étienne-Marcel.* Ever since its construction in 8C, this has always been the busiest and richest of shopping streets. It was the route taken by kings in order to reach Notre-Dame. They have since been replaced by sex shops... Number

Centre Pompidou, designed by Richard Rogers and Renzo Piano

145 leads to the **passage couvert du Grand-Cerf**★ via **rue Tiquetonne** (ⓒ*Quartier 8*).

Fontaine des Innocents★ – ⓜ *Châtelet-Les Halles.* A Renaissance (16C.) masterpiece which was transported in 1786 from the cemetery known as the Saints-Innocents to its present location. Today the fountain peers down on hip-hop fans.

Centre Pompidou - Musée National d'Art Moderne★★★ – ⓜ *Rambuteau - www.centrepompidou.fr - 11h-21h - closed Tue - €14.* Built on the Beaubourg plateau, this astonishing construction with its steel structure, lifts, brightly-painted air and water ducts on the outside, was designed by architects Richard Rogers and Renzo Piano. Inaugurated in 1977, it houses one of the best collections of modern art in the world (nearly 60 000 art works), that explores the evolution of art from early 20C (fauvism, cubism) to the present day. From the top floor there is a superb view over the rooftops of Paris.

WHERE TO EAT

② **Ambassade d'Auvergne** – *22 r. du Grenier-St-Lazare - ⓜ Rambuteau - ☏ 01 42 72 31 22 - www.ambassade-auvergne.com - main courses €18-27.* Serves traditional Auvergne dishes: dry cured sausage, green lentils and must-have Aligot.

WHERE TO EAT

🍴 A change of scenery? Head for the **marché des Enfants-Rouges** 🍴 which will take you on a trip from Japan to the Antilles via Italy *(39 r. de Bretagne - closed Sun evening and Mon)*.

🍴 **Café Charlot** – *38 r. de Bretagne - 🚇 Filles-du-Calvaire - 📞 01 44 54 03 30 - www.cafecharlotparis.com - main courses €15-25*. Within the walls of an old bakery sits a chic, trendy bistrot.

🍴 **Les Philosophes** – *28 r. Vieille-du-Temple - 🚇 St-Paul - 📞 01 48 87 49 64 cafeine.com - salads €11-17, main courses €20-29*. This large bistrot has a relaxed atmosphere and favours organic ingredients used with flair.

🍴 **L'As du Fallafel** – *34 r. des Rosiers - 🚇 St-Paul - closed Fri dinner and Sat - less than €10*. Inexpensive and delicious falafel sandwiches. Be prepared for a long queue. Eat in or take away.

🍴 **Minh Chau** – *10 r. de la Verrerie - 🚇 Hôtel-de-Ville - 📞 01 42 71 13 30 - closed Sun - main courses €5-10*. This tiny Vietnamese canteen serves simple, toothsome fare at low prices.

TAKE A BREAK

🍴 **La Boutique Jaune** – *27 r. des Rosiers - 🚇 St-Paul - closed Tue*. This is Old World Jewish cuisine at its best: bagels, hearty sandwiches, and sweets like strudel. Eat in or take away.

🍴 **L'Ébouillanté** – *6 r. des Barres - 🚇 Pont-Marie*. There is home-made fare on the menu at this tea room. it has a pleasant outdoor terrace.

SHOPPING

🛍 The Parisian shopping mecca, the Marais is home to international fashion labels, jewellery and accessories, designer boutiques, and fine food stores. The **rues des Francs-Bourgeois** and **Vieille-du-Temple** are both especially lively streets. Most stores are open on Sundays.

🛍 **Fleux** – *39 et 52 r. Ste-Croix-de-la-Bretonnerie - 🚇 Hôtel-de-Ville - closed Sun morning*. An ultra-popular concept-store which sells decorative objects, tableware, and furniture. Designer or kitsch, vintage or ultra-modern, there's something here for everyone!

🛍 **Épicerie Izrael** – *30 r. François-Miron - 🚇 St-Paul - closed Sun-Mon*. You can find anything in this Capharnaüm. Worth a visit.

🛍 **Mariage Frères** – *30 r. du Bourg-Tibourg - 🚇 Hôtel-de-Ville*. A haven for connoisseurs with a vast choice of teas. Also has a tea room.

NIGHTLIFE

🎭 **Café de la Gare** – *41 r. du Temple - 🚇 Hôtel-de-Ville - www.cdlg.org*. The theater where Coluche and the Splendid troupe first performed. Chuckle at the comedy plays and *one-man-shows*.

🎭 **Le Pop In** – *105 r. Amelot - 🚇 St-Sébastien-Froissart - from 18h30*. Situated on the festive rue Amelot, this pop rock bar-pub has comfy sofas and live music.

Entries appear in the neighboring quartier:
🍴 🍴 🍴 🍴 🛍 ▶ *3*
🍴 ▶ *11*

The Marais has preserved its medieval streets, squares and 17C and 18C mansions. However, its remarkable historic buildings are now occupied by art galleries, bustling cafés, chic boutiques, and gay bars, transforming the Marais into an ultra-trendy district.

VISIT

Place des Vosges

Église Saint-Paul-Saint-Louis★★ – ⓜ *St-Paul*. Built between 1627 and 1641, this church is a fine example of Baroque architecture. Inside there is a captivating Virgin of Sorrows sculpted by Germain Pilon.

Maison européenne de la Photographie★ – *5-7 r. de Fourcy* - ⓜ *St-Paul* - www.mep-fr.org - *11h-20h - closed Mon-Tue - €8*. The MEP collection comprises over 12 000 photos dating from 1958, presented in temporary exhibitions.

Hôtel de Sens★ – *1 r. du Figuier* - ⓜ *St-Paul*. This 1507 building houses the **Forney library**, which specializes in art and industrial techniques.

Hôtel de Sully★ – *62 r. St-Antoine* - ⓜ *St-Paul*. This Louis XIII style (17C) mansion house is closed to the public, but you can walk through the inner courtyard and garden *(9h-19h)*, to reach the Place des Vosges.

Place des Vosges★★★ – ⓜ *St-Paul*. *(10h-18h - closed Mon - free except for temporary exhibitions)*. Among Paris's most beautiful squares, built under the reign of Henri IV. The brick and stone buildings retain their original features. Once the home of **Victor Hugo**, number 6 is now a museum.

Rue des Francs-Bourgeois★ – ⓜ *St-Paul, Rambuteau*. The central axis of the Marais, lined with shops and mansions from the 16C and 17C (numbers 31, 26, 30.).

Musée Cognacq-Jay★★ – *8 r. Elzévir* - ⓜ *Chemin-Vert* - www.museecognacqjay. paris.fr - *10h-18h - closed Mon - free (except for temporary exhibitions)*. One of the most charming museums in the capital, this collection of 18C European art recalls the Age of Enlightenment.

Musée Picasso★★ – *5 r. de Thorigny* - ⓜ *St-Sébastien-Froissart* - www.musee picassoparis.fr - *11h30-18h, w.-end 9h30-18h - €12.50*. The **Hôtel Salé** (17C) provides the perfect setting for the best collection of this prolific artist's works.

Hôtel de Soubise-Clisson★★ – *60 r. des Francs-Bourgeois* - ⓜ *Rambuteau* - www.archives-nationales.culture.gouv.fr - *10h-17h30, w.-end 14h-17h30 - closed Tue - €8*. Built in 14C, and later greatly altered, this mansion houses the **musée des Archives nationales**. Look out for the vast cour d'honneur and the Rococo style apartments.

Hôtel de Guénégaud★★ – *60-62 r. des Archives* - ⓜ *Rambuteau*. Built around 1650 and remodelled in 18C, this is one of the most beautiful houses in the Marais. Along with the hôtel de Mongelas (18C), it houses the unusual **musée de la Chasse et de la Nature★★** *(Tue-Sun 11h-18h - €8)*.

Musée d'Art et d'Histoire du Judaïsme★★ – *71 r. du Temple* - ⓜ *Rambuteau* - www.mahj.org - *11h-18h (Wed 21h), Sun 10h-18h - closed Sat - €9*. Discover Jewish culture in this modern, educational museum housed in the Hôtel de Saint-Aignan mansion house.

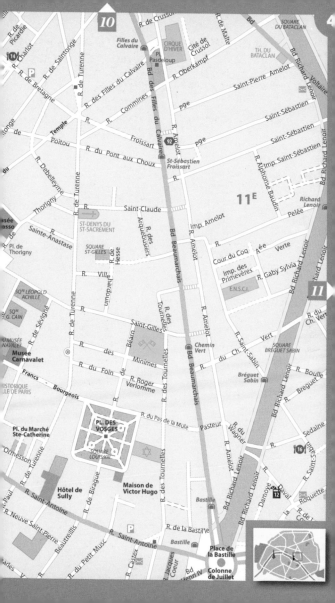

WHERE TO EAT

Ⓐ Montparnasse Quartier is brimming with crêperies, especially along **rues du Montparnasse** and **d'Odessa** (Ⓜ *Montparnasse-Bienvenüe*).

23 L'Altro – *16 r. du Dragon* - Ⓜ *St-Germain-des-Prés* - ☏ *01 45 48 49 49* - *main courses* €20-30. Italian à la carte in a New York bistrot setting.

24 Fish La Boissonnerie – *69 r. de Seine* - Ⓜ *Odéon* - ☏ *01 43 54 34 69* - *menus* €15 (lunch), €32-35 (dinner). Bistrot menu of fish, with some steaks, too.

51 La Ferrandaise – *8 r. de Vaugirard* - Ⓜ *Odéon* - ☏ *01 42 26 36 36* - *www.laferrandaise.com - closed Mon lunch, Sat lunch and Sun - lunch menu* €16, *dinner menus* €37-55. The owner concocts home-made terrines and blanquette from Ferrandaise suckling calf.

39 L'Avant-Comptoir – *3 carr. de l'Odéon* - Ⓜ *Odéon* - ☏ *01 41 01 01 01* - *around* €15. Inspired by tapas bars, chef Yves Camdeborde's convivial eatery has no tables, just a long bar where everyone eats standing up.

65 Le Nemrod – *51 r. du Cherche-Midi* - Ⓜ *Sèvres-Babylone* - ☏ *01 45 48 17 05* - *main courses* €12-18. A beautiful terrace and Auvergne specialties are the choice pick at this convivial brasserie.

TAKE A BREAK

1 Au Sauvignon – *80 r. des Sts-Pères* - Ⓜ *Sèvres-Babylone*. The not-to-be-missed wine bar of the quartier. Serves big, open sandwiches of foie gras, salmon, or cured meat.

10 Ciel de Paris – *Tour Montparnasse* - *33 av. du Maine* - Ⓜ *Montparnasse-Bienvenüe*. A champagne bar with a view, on the 56th floor of Montparnasse Tower.

22 Le Café de Flore – *172 bd St-Germain* - Ⓜ *St-Germain-des-Prés*. Apollinaire, Camus, Sartre and

Beauvoir have all frequented this café opened at the end of 19C.

30 Les Deux Magots – *6 pl. St-Germain-des-Prés* - Ⓜ *St-Germain-des-Prés*. The quartier's other institution, where Verlaine, Rimbaud, Picasso and Hemingway often dropped in.

35 Ladurée – *21 r. Bonaparte* - Ⓜ *St-Germain-des-Prés*. This macaron specialist has a lovely tea room.

SHOPPING

Ⓐ A mecca for savvy fashionistas, Saint-Germain and Montparnasse have great stores, from ready-to-wear (**rue de Rennes**) to haute couture (**bd Saint-Germain**). The historic heart of Parisian literary life, Saint-Germain has several **bookstores**, such as **L'Écume des Pages** **74** (*174 bd St-Germain*).

80 Brand Bazar – *33 r. de Sèvres* - Ⓜ *Sèvres-Babylone - closed Sun.* A well-stocked multi-brand store that offers young, sharp feminine fashion.

57 Épicerie du Bon Marché – *24 r. de Sèvres* - Ⓜ *Sèvres-Babylone - closed Sun.* Offering 30 000 products from all over the globe and a remarkable selection of wines.

Entries appear in the neighboring quartier:
63 **75** **76** **89** ▶ *1*
6 **72** ▶ *6*

Historically Saint-Germain-des-Prés was the haunt for fervent intellectuals and Montparnasse was a favorite with avant-garde artists. Today, much changed, the charm lives on in designer stores, bookshops and famous cafés, which were the hangouts for the great minds of the 20C.

VISIT

Place Saint-Sulpice

Quartier de l'Odéon★★ – ⓜ *Odéon.* Centred around the neoclassical architecture of the **Théâtre de l'Odéon**, built in 1782, the quartier is packed with old bookstores, art galleries, and boutiques. The lively **carrefour de l'Odéon** is surrounded by cinemas and bustling cafés.

Église Saint-Germain-des-Prés★★ – ⓜ *St-Germain-des-Prés.* Originally the site of an important abbey founded in the 6C, this ancient church has been rebuilt several times. The facade's massive tower is the only remaining vestige of earlier times (lthe spire dates from 19C).

Rue de Furstenberg – ⓜ *St-Germain-des-Prés.* Situated on the shady square of this peaceful street is the **musée Delacroix★**, housed in the painter's apartment and studio, where he lived from 1858 to 1863 (6 r. de Furstenberg - 9h30-17h - closed Tue - €5).

Place Saint-Sulpice★★ – ⓜ *St-Sulpice.* This fountain, in the middle of the 18C square, was erected in honor of famous eloquent 17C bishops whose statues appear in the four niches (Bossuet, Massillon, Fléchier, Fénelon).

Église Saint-Sulpice★★ – ⓜ *St-Sulpice.* Founded in 12C, the church has been rebuilt several times, and was extended over 16C and 17C. Its pipe organ (1776) is the largest in France. The Saints-Anges chapel was decorated by Delacroix (1849-1861).

Palais du Luxembourg★★ – *RER B Luxembourg.* Designed by Salomon de Brosse for the queen Marie de Médicis, in early 17C, the palace is now seat to the Senate. The former orangerie, houses the **musée du Luxembourg** which holds popular themed exhibitions.

Jardin du Luxembourg★★ – ⓜ *N.-D.-des-Champs, RER B Luxembourg.* This formal French garden is admired for its harmonious perspectives and shady alleys. The **Médicis fountain★**, at the end of the small lake, is the park's most splendid vestige in honor of Marie de Médicis.

Montparnasse★ – ⓜ *Montparnasse-Bienvenüe.* This neighborhood became legendary when artists and writers began to frequent here in 1900. Some of the artists' studios are now museums : **musée Zadkine★** (100 bis r. d'Assas - 10h-18h - closed Mon - free except for temporary exhibitions), **musée Bourdelle★** (18 r. Antoine-Bourdelle - same as musée Zadkine). Today, visitors come to Montparnasse to see a film, and eat a crêpe at the foot of the highest **tower★** in Paris (access to the summit: 9h30-23h30, winter 22h30 - €15).

Cimetière du Montparnasse – ⓜ *Montparnasse-Bienvenüe.* Covering 19 ha this is Paris' second intra-muros necropolis, after Père-Lachaise. Artists, writers and intellectuals rest here, including Baudelaire, Sartre and Gainsbourg.

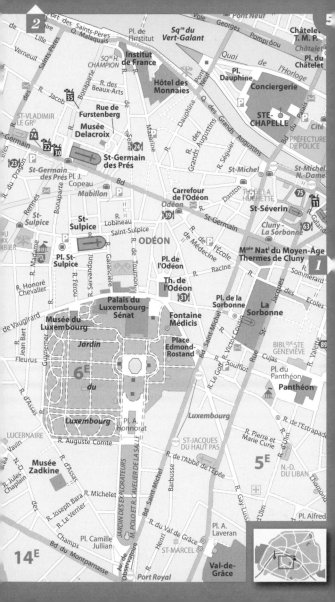

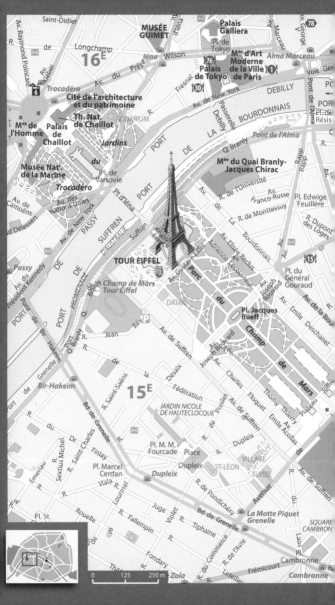

performances, projections, concerts, dance... there's always something to do or see at the Palais de Tokyo!

WHERE TO EAT

6 New York – *6 av. de New-York* - ⓜ *Alma-Marceau* - ☏ *01 40 70 03 30* - *www.6newyork.fr* - *closed Sat lunch and Sun* - *main courses €25-35*. This chic bistrot concocts a cuisine in harmony with its décor: Modern and refined.

Au Pied de Fouet – *45 r. de Babylone* - ⓜ *St-François-Xavier, Vaneau* - ☏ *01 47 05 12 27* - *closed Sun* - *main courses €13-20*. Unpretentious cuisine served in an authentic Parisian bistrot atmosphere and keenly priced.

Café Constant – *139 r. St-Dominique* - ⓜ *École-Militaire* - ☏ *01 47 53 73 34* - *www.maisonconstant.com* - *main courses €16-28*. A convivial Christian Constant annex, serving savoury bistrot dishes such as eggs mimosa, roast lamb and rice pudding at reasonable prices.

Les Marches – *5 r. de la Manutention* - ⓜ *Iéna* - ☏ *01 47 23 52 80* - *www.lesmarches-restaurant.com* - *main courses €14-22*. French food from days of yore, including steak Bearnaise, eggs *meurette* (poached in red wine sauce) and sweets like pear sorbet.

L'Affriolé – *17 r. Malar* - ⓜ *Invalides* - ☏ *01 85 15 24 65* - *www.laffriole.fr* - *closed Sun-Mon* - *main courses €25* - *menus €39-65*. Chalked-up daily specials and a menu of the month. The chef show-cases market-fresh produce. The lunchtime, fixed price 'Bento' menu (€19) is perfect for those in a rush.

Café du Marché – *38 r. Cler* - ⓜ *École-Militaire* - ☏ *01 47 05 51 27* - *www.cafe-du-marche.fr* - *closed Sun evening* - *main courses €10-15*. A local favourite, serving big tasty French fare.

Tokyo Eat

Tokyo Eat – *Palais de Tokyo - 13 av. du Prés.-Wilson* - ⓜ *Iéna* - ☏ *01 47 20 00 29* - *main courses €15-25*. A surprisingly arty cuisine is served in this hip, creative hotspot: courgettes marinated with garlic petals, strips of raw tuna with sake and oil of mint.

TAKE A BREAK

Café Central – *40 r. Cler* - ⓜ *École-Militaire*. An immense terrace on a pleasant, pedestrian street.

Carette – *4 pl. du Trocadéro* - ⓜ *Trocadéro*. An old-fashioned, historic tea room with service to match. Teatime choices include tart tatin, macarons and chocolate eclairs. There are salads are on the menu for lunch.

SHOPPING

The **avenue Montaigne** (ⓜ *Alma-Marceau*), lined with luxury stores and upscale apartments, simply oozes with elegance. It is the ideal spot for window shopping.

Quatrehomme – *62 r. de Sèvres* - ⓜ *Vaneau* - *closed Sun-Mon*. This cheesemaker, who has been awarded the 'Meilleur Ouvrier de France' title, takes you on an unforgettable culinary tour of France.

Entries appear in quartier 7:

Within sight of the famous silhouette of the Tour Eiffel, museums and monuments abound between the Invalides and the Trocadéro. Nearby, the Guimet and Quai Branly museums house treasures brought back from far-away expeditions.

VISIT

Pont Alexandre-III★★ – 🚇 *Invalides.* Since 7 October 1896, the date when the first stone was laid by Tsar Nicolas II, this bridge has symbolized the ties between France and Russia.

Hôtel des Invalides★★★ – 🚇 *Invalides - www.musee-armee.fr - 10h-18h (winter 17h) - €11/12.* Built in 1671 to treat the war-wounded, today it is home to diverse military authorities and the **musée de l'Armée★★★**. At the centre of its facade, an archway, modelled on the Arc de Triomphe, leads to the cour d'honneur and the **église Saint-Louis-des-Invalides ★**. On the other side, the **église du Dôme★★★** (1677-1706), constructed by Jules Hardouin-Mansart, houses the tomb of Napoléon I.

Musée Rodin★★ – *79 r. de Varenne -* 🚇 *Varenne - www.musee-rodin.fr - 10h-17h45 (Wed 20h45) - closed Mon - €10.* In the **Hôtel Biron★★** (18C), where Auguste Rodin lived from 1908, admire displays of the sculptor's works: *Le Penseur, Les Bourgeois de Calais, La Porte de l'Enfer.* Sculptures are scattered all around the beautiful garden.

Tour Eiffel★★★ – 🚇 *Bir-Hakeim, RER C Champ-de-Mars-Tour-Eiffel - www.toureiffel.paris - 9h30-23h (summer 9h-0h) - 7-17 €10/16 (fl. 2), €19/25 (top) .* The iron tower, built by Gustave Eiffel in the 1889, peers down onto the capital from a height of 364 m. From the summit (access by lift or by climbing 1 652 steps), the panorama stretches over 67 km on a clear day.

Hôtel des Invalides with the église du Dôme

Palais de Chaillot★★ – 🚇 *Trocadéro.* Built for the 1937 Universal Exhibition it is home to the **musée de l'Homme★** (www.museedelhomme.fr - 11h-18h, Wed 21h - closed Tue - €10) and the **Cité de l'architecture et du patrimoine★★** (www.citechaillot.fr - 11h-19h, Thu 21h - closed Tue - €8). The **parvis des Droits de l'Homme** leads to a terrace which offers a sweeping view of the Eiffel Tower. Spread out below are the **jardins du Trocadéro★★**.

Musée du Quai Branly-Jacques Chirac★★ – *37 quai Branly -* 🚇 *Alma-Marceau, RER C Pont-de-l'Alma - www.quaibranly.fr - 11h-19h (Thu-Sat 21h) - closed Mon - €10.* Designed by Jean Nouvel, this building is home to around 3 500 exhibits which take you on a voyage to Oceania, America, Africa and Asia.

Musée Guimet★★★ – *Pl. d'Iéna -* 🚇 *Iéna - www.guimet.fr - 10h-18h - closed Tue - €8.50/11.50.* This museum is reputed to have the richest collection of Asiatic art, from Khmer treasures to Japanese prints, from Chinese porcelain to Gandhara Buddhas.

Musée d'Art moderne de la Ville de Paris★★ – *11 av. du Prés.-Wilson -* 🚇 *Iéna - www.mam.paris.fr - 10h-18h (Thu 22h) - closed Mon - free (except for temporary exhibitions).* This rich collection runs from 20C avant-garde artists to conceptual Europeans.

Palais de Tokyo★ – *13 av. du Prés.-Wilson -* 🚇 *Iéna - www.palaisdetokyo.com - 12h-0h - closed Tue - €12.* Exhibitions,

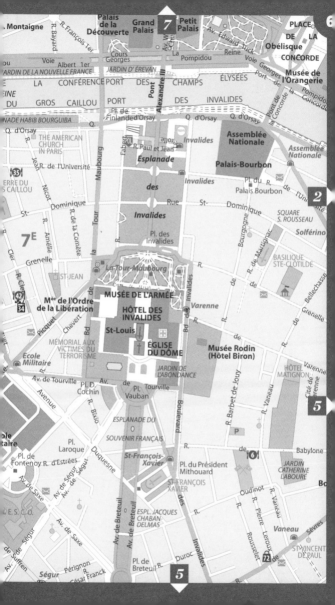

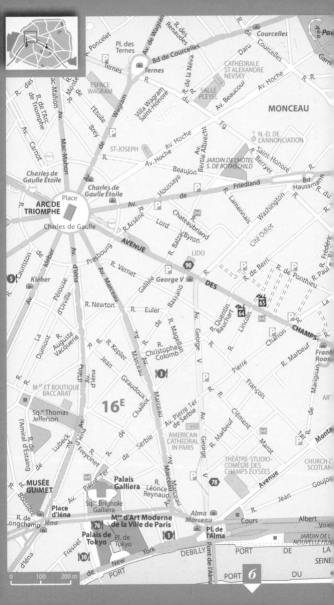

WHERE TO EAT

🟦5 Atelier Vivanda – 18 r. Lauriston - 🚇 Kléber - ☎ 01 40 67 10 00 - www.atelier vivanda.com - closed weekend - menu €36. Chef Akrame Benallal prepares food for carnivores: Black Angus beef, farm-reared chicken, duck, and Iberian pork. Butcher's blocks serve as tables.

🟦5 Le Maxan – 3 r. Quentin-Bauchart - 🚇 George-V - ☎ 01 40 70 04 78 - www. rest-maxan.com - closed Sat lunch and Sun - menus €32-42. An elegant restaurant, decorated in monochrome gray with market-driven dishes.

🟦34 Pomze – 109 bd Haussmann - 🚇 Miromesnil, St-Augustin - ☎ 01 42 65 65 83 - www.pomze.com - closed Sat lunch and Sun - menu €36. Enjoy creative dishes prepared with apples. Original cider-food matches are proposed. There is also a grocery store.

🟦74 Swoon's – 10 r. des Saussaies - 🚇 Madeleine, Miromesnil - ☎ 01 42 68 00 02 - closed eves and weekends - main courses €8-12. A small eatery serving sandwiches, salads and daily specials.

TAKE A BREAK

🟦3 Buddha Bar – 8 r. Boissy-d'Anglas - 🚇 Concorde. Popular place to eat under the gaze of a giant Buddha. Ideal for a post-sightseeing cocktail.

🟦4 Café Jacquemart-André – 158 bd Haussmann - 🚇 Miromesnil - closed eve. The menu in the dining room of the Jacquemart-André mansion house includes tea, ice cream and pastries. For lunch there are salads and daily specials.

🟦64 Ladurée – 75 av. des Champs-Élysées - 🚇 George-V. Treat yourself to delicious macarons, pastries and ice cream in a space kitted out in Napoleon III décor. The restaurant also serves salads and savory dishes. Free WiFi.

Window display, Ladurée

🟦65 86 Champs – 86 av. des Champs-Élysées - 🚇 Charles de Gaulle-Étoile. The tea room-shop of pastry chef/chocolatier Pierre Hermé. A delight!

SHOPPING

🛍 There's everything a shopper could wish for on the **Champs-Élysées**, the longest avenue in Paris. Most stores here are open Sundays.

🟥52 Abercrombie & Fitch – 23 av. des Champs-Élysées - 🚇 Franklin-Roosevelt. A subdued atmosphere, athletic bodies painted on the walls, pop sounds: this American brand has nailed the decor of its only French store.

🟥55 CFOC – 170 bd Haussmann - 🚇 Miromesnil - closed Sun. The Compagnie Française de l'Orient et de la Chine sells furniture, lights, linens and tableware.

NIGHTLIFE

🎭 Fans of cabaret will find two mythique **Parisian venues** in the Champs-Élysées Quartier: the **Lido** 🟩90 (116 bis av. des Champs-Élysées - 🚇 George-V - www.lido.fr) and the **Crazy Horse** 🟩75 (12 av. George-V - 🚇 Alma-Marceau - www.lecrazyhorseparis.com).

🟩91 Le Showcase – Pont Alexandre-III - 🚇 Champs-Élysées-Clemenceau. This former boat shed, under the Alexandre-III bridge, is now a club.

Entries appear in quartier 6: 🟦101 🟥76

Stretching from the place de la Concorde to the Arc de Triomphe, the grandiose Avenue des Champs-Élysées is Paris's most famous boulevard. To the north lies the Monceau quartier where the streets, lined with beautiful Haussmann façades, converge to one of the prettiest parks in western Paris.

Arc de Triomphe

VISIT

Avenue des Champs-Élysées★★★ – ⓜ Champs-Élysées-Clemenceau, Concorde, Charles-de-Gaulle-Étoile.
This is the longest and most famous avenue in Paris (71 m wide and 2 km long). It traces a triumphal route from the place de la Concorde to the Arc de Triomphe. Its cafés, cinemas and shopping arcades are open at all hours.

Arc de Triomphe★★★ – ⓜ Charles-de-Gaulle-Étoile - 10h-23h (winter 22h30) - www.paris-arc-de-triomphe.fr/en - €12.
The design of this monument, built in 1806, was inspired by ancient architecture. It was erected to commemorate Napoleon's victories, and stands in the middle of the place Charles-de-Gaulle, which has 12 avenues radiating out in a star shape. The tomb of the Unknown Soldier lies under the vault of the arch.

Place de la Concorde★★★ – ⓜ Concorde.
The ancient pink granite **Obélisque★** looms over this immense 18C square. It was gifted in 1831 by the viceroy of Egypt, Méhémet Ali.

Grand Palais★ – 3 av. du Gén.-Eisenhower - ⓜ Champs-Élysées-Clemenceau - www.grandpalais.fr - temporary exhibitions €15.
The Grand Palais was built for the 1900 Universal Exhibition and its vast hall is covered with a huge glass roof. The National Galleries, with 5 000 m² of floor space, host themed temporary art exhibitions.

Petit Palais★★ – Av. Winston-Churchill - ⓜ Champs-Élysées-Clemenceau - www.petit-palais.paris.fr - 10h-18h - closed Mon - free (except temporary exhibitions).
The Petit Palais, which was built at the same time as the Grand Palais, became the Musée des Beaux-Arts de Paris in 1902. The collection showcases French art from 1880 to 1914.

Parc Monceau★ – ⓜ Monceau.
This part-German, part-English garden (1778) has rare species (sycamore maple, Oriental plane, ginkgo biloba) and pretty constructions (colonnade, pyramid, grotto). Luxury mansions overlook the park.

Musée Nissim-de-Camondo★★ – 63 r. de Monceau - ⓜ Monceau - 10h-17h30 - closed Mon-Tue - €9 (€13 Musée des Arts Décoratifs combo ticket).
This lovely mansion house, built in 1914, has a wonderful Belle Époque atmosphere. The museum displays the sumptuous furnishings and décor chosen by its former owner, Count de Camondo.

Musée Cernuschi★ – 7 av. Velasquez - ⓜ Monceau - www.cernuschi.paris.fr - 10h-18h - closed Mon - free (except temporary exhibitions).
The museum, which was founded by Henri Cernuschi in late 19C, has a fine collection of Asian art.

Musée Jacquemart-André★★ – 158 bd Haussmann - ⓜ Miromesnil - www.musee-jacquemart-andre.com - 10h-18h - €13.50.
This mansion, built in 1869, houses a collection of 18C decorative art and paintings: Boucher, Chardin, Fragonard, Rembrandt.

WHERE TO EAT

(13) **Brasserie Gallopin** - *40 r. N.-D.-des-Victoires - Bourse - 01 42 36 45 38 - www.brasseriegallopin.com - main courses €19-35.* This restaurant, which opened in 1876, has a stunning Belle Epoque décor with zinc, mahogany, and a 1900 glass veranda. The menu features classic brasserie dishes.

(19) **Chartier** - *7 r. du Fbg-Montmartre - Grands-Boulevards - 01 47 70 86 29 - www.bouillon-chartier.com - main courses €8.50-13.50.* This authentic Parisian bistrot was established in 1896. The dining room is a relic of the past.

(25) **Guibine** - *44 r. Ste-Anne - Quatre-Septembre - 01 40 20 45 83 - closed Mon - main courses €15-18.* A Korean restaurant serving delicious *bulgogi* (barbecue), *bibimbap*, seaweed and fermented lotus root.

(58) **L'Office** - *3 r. Richer - Bonne-Nouvelle - 01 47 70 67 31 - closed w.-end - menus €22-32.* A hidden gem, this bistrot serves market-driven, well-priced cuisine.

(79) **Pascade** - *14 r. Daunou - Opéra - 01 42 60 11 00 - pascade-alexandre-bourdas.com - main courses around €20.* The chef pays tribute to Aveyron with his speciality: the *pascade*, a pancake with a savoury or sweet filling.

TAKE A BREAK

(31) **Café de la Paix** - *5 pl. de l'Opéra - Opéra.* Since 1862, the terrace of this opulent restaurant has been the place to people-watch and look out at the florid Palais Garnier, Charles Garnier's Opera house.

SHOPPING

A shopping trip to the **department stores** is essential. **Printemps** (71) and **Galeries Lafayette** (58), which opened in late 19C, stock international designer labels. *(40 and 64 bd Haussmann - Havre-Caumartin - closed Sundays).* Nearby, in the **Citadium** (81) there is a vast choice of urban fashion *(56 r. de Caumartin - closed Sun).* On another level, discover quirky, old-fashioned boutiques in the **passages couverts**. (*Visit*).

Chartier

(82) **À la Mère de Famille** - *35 r. du Fbg-Montmartre - Grands-Boulevards - closed Sun afternoon.* This is the oldest candy store in Paris. Feast your eyes on the array of chocolates, jams and confectionary displayed behind the traditional wooden storefront.

(29) **Legrand Filles et Fils** - *Galerie Vivienne, 1 r. de la Banque - Bourse - closed Sun.* This appealing wine and fine food store is located in the Vivienne arcade. Table d'hôte meals are served at lunchtime.

NIGHTLIFE

(72) **Rex Club** - *5 bd Poissonnière - Bonne-Nouvelle - www.rexclub.com - Thu-Sat.* Iconic Parisian club with famed DJs on the decks.

(77) **Harry's New York Bar** - *5 r. Daunou - Opéra.* The Bloody Mary was invented in this mythical piano bar, opened in 1911, and made famous by writers such as Hemingway. opened in 1911, and made famous by writers such as Hemingway.

Entries appear in the neighboring quartier:

(9) (26) (64) (36) (56) ▶ 2
(77) (74) ▶ 3

This cultural neighborhood is home to the Opéra, and the Grands Boulevards theaters. Avid shoppers are drawn to the place Vendôme and the renowned department stores. Take time to stroll through the charming covered passageways, packed with boutiques and restaurants.

VISIT

Église de la Madeleine★ –

Madeleine. The 52, 20m-high majestic columns surrounding this church give it the appearance of a Greek temple. Its construction began in 1764 and the church was consecrated in 1842. The pediment sculpture on the facade of the Last Judgement is by Lemaire.

Rue Saint-Honoré★ – Madeleine.

Stroll along this long, busy street, teeming with high-end boutiques. Admire the few remaining ancient storefronts (nos 209 and 211).

Place Vendôme★★ – Opéra.

Jules Hardouin-Mansart designed this square, once graced by an equestrian statue of Louis XIV. The **colonne d'Austerlitz** now stands in its place. Today, luxury reigns here: the square has become a smart address for exclusive jewellery boutiques.

Rue de la Paix – Opéra. This

elegant street has become renowned for high-end jewellery stores, such as Cartier, Mauboussin and Bulgari.

Palais Garnier - Opéra national de Paris★★ – Opéra - www.operade
paris.fr - 10h-17h - (summer 17h30) - www.
operadeparis.fr/en - €11. This Second Empire building was designed by Charles Garnier in 1860. The magnificent grand staircase of honour, the sumptuous foyer with a ceiling by Chagall, and the prestigious ballet company are all worthwhile reasons to visit the Opéra.

Galerie Vivienne

Avenue de l'Opéra★ – Opéra,
Pyramide. This avenue, created between 1854 and 1878, has become a shopping paradise, with shops selling scarves, perfume, and gifts.

Grands Boulevards – Richelieu-
Drouot, Grands-Boulevards. In the 19C this was a chic, artistic spot to stroll, today the **boulevards des Italiens**, **Montmartre** and **Poissonnière** are brimming with cinemas and restaurants. The **Grand Rex** cinema (1932) which is one of the oldest, is worth a look.

Les passages★ – The 19C
covered passageways have their own special atmosphere. Under the high glass roof are restaurants, cafés and shops. Take a look at the **galeries Vivienne et Colbert★★** (4-6 r. des Petits-Champs et 2-6 r. Vivienne), the **passages des Panoramas** (enter via 151 r. Montmartre and 11 bd Montmartre), **Jouffroy** (10 bd Montmartre), **Verdeau** (6 r. de la Grange-Batelière), **des Princes** (5 bd des Italiens - closed Sun), **du Caire★** (pl. du Caire - closed w.-end) and **du Grand-Cerf★** (r. Dussoubs and St-Denis - closed Sun).

Musée Grévin★ – 10 bd Montmartre -
Grands-Boulevards - www.grevin-paris.com - 10h-18h30 - €22.50 (discount if booked in advance). Visitors come here to meet their idols: over the last 100 years, 2000 wax figures have been featured.

[28] Jeanne B – 61 r. Lepic - 🚇 Blanche-Abbesses - 📞 01 42 51 17 53 - www.jeanne-b-comestibles.com - menus €19-29. A friendly restaurant/grocery store serving simple bistrot fare.

[43] Le Café Qui Parle – 24 r. Caulaincourt - 🚇 Lamarck-Caulaincourt, Blanche - 📞 01 46 06 06 88 - cafequiparle. fr/en- closed Sun evening - main courses €18-25. Tuck into modern French food, like a salad of fried goat cheese, smoked duck and caramelised pear.

[56] L'Été en Pente Douce – 23 r. Muller - 🚇 Anvers, Château-Rouge - 📞 01 42 64 02 67 - www.parisresto.com - main courses €10-18. A restaurant-tea room on the Butte with ample outdoor seating. Salads, cold platters and pastries make up the menu.

[82] Le Restaurant – 32 r. Véron - 🚇 Blanche - 📞 01 42 23 06 22 - www. lerestaurant-montmartre.fr - menu €25. A popular neighbourhood eatery that prepares unpretentious bistrot dishes using quality produce.

TAKE A BREAK

[59] Gontran Cherrier – 22 r. Caulaincourt - 🚇 Lamarck-Caulaincourt, Blanche - closed Wed. Head to the hottest bakery in town to feast on fresh baguettes, foccacias, croissants and pastries.

[15] La Fourmi – 74 r. des Martyrs - 🚇 Pigalle. Come evenings, this lovely bar, decorated with flea-market finds, fills up with a lively young crowd.

SHOPPING

[60] Marché Saint-Pierre – 2 r. Charles-Nodier - 🚇 Anvers -closed Sun. People come from afar to stock up at this gigantic six-storey fabric market.

[62] La Petite Maroquinerie – 16 r. Houdon - 🚇 Abbesses, Pigalle. A store selling original, quality leather goods at reasonable prices.

[54] Cosi Loti – 21 r. Houdon - 🚇 Pigalle, Abbesses - closed Mon. Stocked with a home and fashion accessories, this is the place to pick up a throw cushion, dainty jewellery, or pastel tableware.

NIGHTLIFE

🍸 Head for **SoPi** and stop for a drink on the rue Jean-Baptiste Pigalle, at r. Henry-Monnier or r. Frochot, at one of the many hipster places that have replaced the hostess bars.

[73] Bus Palladium – 6 r. Fontaine - 🚇 Pigalle - www.lebuspalladium.com. A club and rock concert venue that has become mythical since its opening in 1965. In the evenings there is an American restaurant.

[14] La Divette de Montmartre – 136 r. Marcadet - 🚇 Lamarck-Caulaincourt. A typical 70s Parisian bar dedicated to rock, with live music on Fridays.

[86] Le Glass – 7 r. Frochot - 🚇 Pigalle - from 19h30. There is a short but well-curated list of cocktails and beers at this trendy, low-key bar.

[94] Machine du Moulin-Rouge – 90 bd de Clichy - 🚇 Blanche - www.lamachi-nedumoulin-rouge.com. This urban-style club is good for dancing.

[37] Vingt Heures Vin – 17 r. Joseph-de-Maistre - 🚇 Blanche - from 19h. This popular wine bar has ample bottles and glasses to match the cheese and charcuterie platters.

© Till Jacket / Photononstop

Through the crowds of tourists at Montmartre, you can still see traces of village life, with paved streets, artists studios and a small vineyard which turns its back to the immense white-domed Sacré-Cœur. Spreading out below are the lively quartiers of Pigalle and the trendy SoPi.

Basilique du Sacré-Cœur

VISIT

Montmartre★★★ – ⓜ *Anvers, Abbesses.* Climb up the rue Lepic, until you reach the **moulin de la Galette**, which was a 19C dance hall venue. In the early 20C the **Bateau-Lavoir** (*n° 13*), situated on the pretty **place Émile-Goudeau★**, was a lively meeting place for painters and poets. Another hotspot for the bohemian Montmartre society was the **Lapin Agile** which sits at the crossroads of the rue Saint-Vincent and the rue des Saules, bordered by a tiny **vineyard**. Each year, the wine harvest is celebrated by a fun-packed festival.

Place des Abbesses★ – ⓜ *Abbesses.* The Abbesses Métro station's entrance (kiosk), designed by Hector Guimard, is one of only two left in Paris (the other is at Porte Dauphine). The original **Saint-Jean-de-Montmartre** church was the first religious building to be constructed with reinforced concrete (1904).

Place du Tertre★ – ⓜ *Abbesses.* In the morning, before the square fills up with artists, portrait painters and tourists, the place du Tertre, lined with small houses and trees, has a villagey feel.

Église Saint-Pierre-de-Montmartre★ – ⓜ *Abbesses.* This ancient church (1134), the only relic remaining of Montmartre abbey, has a curious mixture of architectural styles. The three bronze doors were sculpted by Gismondi in 1980.

Sacré-Cœur★★ – ⓜ *Anvers et funiculaire de Montmartre.* This famous white silhouette is part of the Paris skyline. The Roman-Byzantine basilica (1876-1914) was built by the architect Paul Abadie. Visitors can climb the 300 steps to the dome (*€6*); and admire the stunning view over the church's interior from the inside gallery, and over Paris from the outside gallery.

Pigalle – ⓜ *Pigalle.* South of the Montmartre Butte sits Pigalle. The seedy reputation of this district, once full of crooks and ladies of the night, has been taken over by cabaret shows and hip cafés, although a few sleazy sex shops and strip-tease joints still exist. The **boulevard de Clichy** joins Pigalle to the place Blanche where the **Moulin-Rouge**, the most famous cabaret in Paris, has stood since 1889 (*www.moulin rouge.com*).

The **South Pigalle** neighborhood, around the **rue des Martyrs**, has been newly dubbed as **SoPi.** The area has been populated by a wave of clubs, hipster bars and restaurants, organic and vintage stores.

WHERE TO EAT

🍽 **Buvette** – *28 r. Henri-Monnier -* ⓜ *Pigalle - ☎ 01 44 63 41 71 - www.ilove buvette.com - closed Mon - price range €25/35.* A laid back gastrothèque serving simple cuisine, in small casserole dishes.

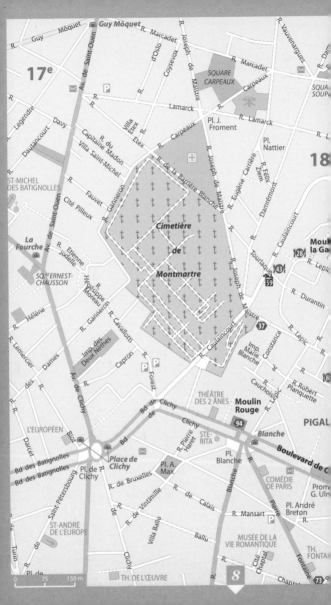

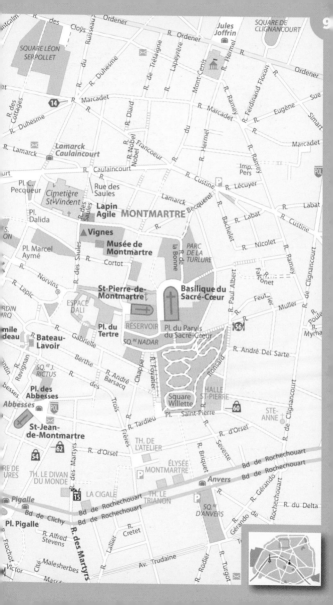

101 Chez Marie-Louise – *111 r. Marie-et-Louise -*  *Goncourt -* 01 53 19 02 04 - *www.chezmarielouise.com - closed Sat lunch and Sun - main courses €17-23.* Select from the chalked-up menu's simple dishes, like steak Béarnaise, herby black pudding, and delicious desserts.

127 Hôtel du Nord – *102 quai de Jemmapes -* Jacques-Bonsergent *-* 01 40 40 78 78 - *www.hoteldunord.org - main courses €15-26.* A retro café-restaurant which featured in Marcel Carné's film *Hôtel du Nord.*

104 Le Camion à Pizzas – *Off map, inside le Centquatre - 5 r. Curial -* Riquet *- 12h-15h, weekend 11h-19h - closed Mon - pizzas €9-12.* In the courtyard of le Centquatre is this food truck serving wood-fire-oven pizzas.

169 Quedubon – *22 r. du Plateau -* Buttes-Chaumont *-* 01 42 38 18 65 - *www.restaurantquedubon.fr - closed Sat lunch, Sun and Mon - main courses €20-30.* This modern bistrot, where the owner likes to play with the flavors, has a wine list showcasing small growers.

178 La Petite Halle – *Parc de La Villette -* Porte-de-Pantin *-* 09 82 25 81 81 - *www.lapetitehalle.com - closed Sun evenings in March - main courses €12-16.* With trendy decor, pizza and cultural events, this place has everything necessary to seduce guests.

TAKE A BREAK

38 La Chambre aux Oiseaux – *48 r. Bichat -* Jacques-Bonsergent *- closed eve and Mon.* This cosy tearoom with retro décor serves delicious cakes and homemade lemonade. They also do lunch, and brunch at the weekend.

19 Péniche Antipode – *55 quai de Seine -* Jaurès. On a barge with a terrace, eat dishes are prepared using products from fair trade sources. Bring the kids for fun performances.

8 Rosa Bonheur – *Parc des Buttes-Chaumont - 2 av. des Cascades -* Botzaris, Buttes-Chaumont *- closed Mon-Tue.* This emblematic open-air dance hall, tucked away in the park, is popular with Parisians.

SHOPPING

53 Antoine & Lili – *95 quai de Valmy -* Jacques-Bonsergent. Behind the three vividly-coloured façades you'll find a store packed with colorful clothes,and ethnic decorative objects.

63 Pop Market – *50 r. Bichat -* Jacques-Bonsergent *- closed Sun.* A store selling gadgets, gifts, decorative objects and lots of other trinkets for both children and adults.

NIGHTLIFE

71 Le Glazart – *7/15 av. Porte de La Villette -* Porte-de-La-Villette *- www.glazart.com.* One of east Paris' essential nightlife locations, with concerts, DJs and a beach in summer (June-Oct).

97 Trabendo – *Parc de La Villette -* Porte-de-Pantin *- www.letrabendo.net.* This famous live music venue proposes an eclectic concert program (rock, electro, hip-hop).

70 Point Éphémère – *200 quai de Valmy -* Jaurès *- www.pointephemere.org.* A trendy warehouse-style bar-restaurant that organizes concerts, exhibitions and shows.

Entries appear in quartier 3: 🔟

© V. Kanazawa/Michelin

A leisurely stroll along the Saint-Martin canal, a remnant of 19C industrial Paris, leads you to the Parc de La Villette. This vast park offers cultural and leisure activites, as well as science and art facilities. A walk to the Buttes-Chaumont or through the Mouzaïa quartier will make a perfect end to the day.

Canal Saint-Martin

VISIT

Canal Saint-Martin★ – *République.* The canal is a charming waterway with nine locks, ironwork footbridges, and shady paved quaysides. On summer evenings, the quays are crowded with picnicking Parisians.

Bassin de La Villette★ – *Jaurès.* This is a good spot to unwind, and has two MK2 cinemas facing each other. It's worth watching the raising of the **swing bridge** on the rue de Crimée, which allows boats to pass from the lake to the canal de l'Ourcq.

Parc de La Villette★ – *Porte-de-la-Villette.* This vast park is a succession of themed gardens and open spaces for playing games. The **Grande Halle** and the **Zénith** host shows and concerts, while 3D-films and documentaries are screened in the stainless steel globe called the **Géode★★** (*www.lageode.fr* - €12).

Cité des Sciences et de l'Industrie★★ – *Porte-de-la-Villette - www.cite-sciences.fr* - 10h-18h (Sun 19h) - closed Sun - €12. This space, created in 1986, is devoted to scientfic culture, and holds educational and fun exhibitions. The hands-on exhibitions in the **Cité des Enfants★★★**, are geared for 2-12 year olds.

Philharmonie de Paris★ – *Porte-de-Pantin -philharmoniedeparis.fr.* The futuristic concert hall designed by Jean Nouvel is a huge carapace covered with mirrors. The

Philharmonie 2, the old Cité de la Musique designed by Christian de Portzamparc, houses the **Musée de la Musique** *(12h-18h, Sun 10h-18h - closed Mon - €8/11),* which showcases a vast panorama of the musical world from 17C to today, through a sonic and visual journey.

Le Centquatre – *Beyond the map range, northwest of the bassin de La Villette - 5 r. Curia - ௫ Riquet - www.104.fr - 12h-19h (weekends 11h-19h) - closed Mon.* This centre, devoted to cultural activities and urban art, holds exhibitions and shows. Watch the neighborhood kids performing hip-hop or capoeira.

Parc des Buttes-Chaumont★ – *௫ Buttes-Chaumont.* Take a pleasant stroll through this park, created in late 19C under Napoléon III's orders. It has a varied landscape with a lake, waterfalls, and gigantic trees.

Quartier de la Mouzaïa★ – *௫ Danube.* A patch of countryside hides between the place de Rhin-et-Danube and place des Fêtes. The tiny streets lined with pretty houses, were inhabited in 19C by quarrymen from the Buttes-Chaumont quarries.

WHERE TO EAT

7 Au Rendez-vous de la Marine – *14 quai de la Loire - ௫ Jaurès - ௫ 01 42 49 33 40 - www.aurendezvousdela marine.fr - closed Sun-Mon- main courses €14-19.* Hearty, value-for-money meals are served in this restaurant.

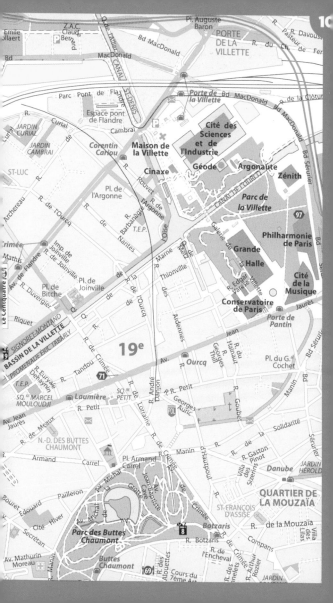

Emile
ollaert

Z.A.C.
Claude
Bernard

Bd

Q. de Tillier

CANAL ST-DENIS

Bd MacDonald

Pl. Auguste
Baron

R. Pasteur Bd Davousx

PORTE
DE LA
VILLETTE

R. du Ch. de Fer

MacDonald

Parc Pont de Flandre

Espace pont de Flandre

Curial

R.

JARDIN
CURIAL

JARDIN
CAMBRAI

ST-LUC

Curial

Cambrai

Porte de
la Villette

Bd MacDonald

de la Clôture

Bd MacDonald

Bd Sérurier

Corentin
Cariou

Maison de
la Villette

Cité des
Sciences
et de
l'Industrie

R.

de

R. de l'Ourcq

Archereau

Pl. de
l'Argonne

Cinaxe

Rouvet

R. de
l'Argonne

Géode

Argonaute

Zénith

T.E.P.

Barbanègre

R. de
Nantes

de

Parc de
la Villette

97

Philharmonie
de Paris

Crimée

Mathis

Av. de Flandre

Imp. de
Joinville
R. de Joinville

Pl. de
Bitche

R. Duvergier

Pl. de
Joinville

de

de la

de l'Ourcq

Thionville

Marne

Q. de
la Marne

Galerie de l'Ourcq

des

R. Edgar
Varèse

Grande

Halle

Cité
de la
Musique

Conservatoire
de Paris

Porte de
Pantin

Jaurès

Le Cinquante (51)

Riquet

SIGNORET-MONTAND

BASSIN DE LA VILLETTE
PROMENADE ÉRIC TABARLY

Q.

R.

de

Crimée

Ardennes

Jean

R. du
Hainaut

Georges
Thill

Av.

Ourcq

19e

Bd Sérurier

Pl. du G.al
Cochet

Manin

Bd Sérurier

R. Euryale
Dehaynin

T.E.P.

SQ.re
MARCEL
MOULOUDJI

Tandou

Laumière

R. Petit

R. Petit

R. André
Danjon

SQ.re
PETIT

R.

de

Lorraine

de

Crimée

Georges
Auric

POL

R.

R. Petit

R.

Goube

Solidarité

Av. Jean
Jaurès

R. de Meaux

N.-D. DES BUTTES
CHAUMONT

Armand

Carrel

Pl. Armand
Carrel

Manin

d'Hautpoul

R.

de

R. Gaston
Pinot

Villa
des
Sizerins

Danube

JARDIN
HÉROLD

Bouret

R.

Édouard

Pailleron

Av. Michal

Grotte

Jean-Baptiste

Av. Michal

Jean-Baptiste

de

Crimée

QUARTIER DE
LA MOUZAÏA

ST-FRANÇOIS
D'ASSISE

R. de la Mouzaïa

Villa
des
Lilas

Cité
Secrétan

Hiver

Av. Michal

Parc des Buttes
Chaumont

8

Botzaris

R. Botzaris

Botzaris

R. de
l'Encheval

Compans

Av. Mathurin
Moreau

Manin

Buttes
Chaumont

69

R. des
Alouettes

Cours du
7ème Art

R. de Crimée

R. des
annelets

R. Arthur
Rozier

JARDIN

Pierre Sang in Oberkampf – *55 r. Oberkampf - Parmentier - 09 67 31 96 80 www.pierresangboyer.com - menus €20-35 (lunch), €39 (dinner) - no reservations.* Here there is a single menu that changes every meal and every day, and the kitchen is expert at accommodating dietary restrictions.

Soya – *20 r. de la Pierre-Levée - Parmentier - 01 48 05 13 00 - closed Sun eve - main courses €16-20.* This is one of the best vegetarian spots, with much of its elegant food gluten-free.

TAKE A BREAK

Kopi Cream – *16 r. Daval - Bastille - closed Mon.* Superb coffee in a snug, bright space. Munch on a thick slice of banana bread or go savoury with quiche. Brunch served at weekends.

La Bellevilloise – *19-21 r. Boyer - Gambetta - www.labellevilloise.com.* This café exudes charm with its potted olive trees and glass roof. It also hosts live music, film screenings, and late-night parties.

La Belle Équipe – *92 r. de Charonne - Faidherbe-Chaligny.* Breakfast, lunch, dinner, and snacks are served at this beloved neighbourhood joint where the staff and food are warm.

SHOPPING

The **rues Paul-Bert**, **Faidherbe** (Faidherbe-Chaligny), and **Keller** (Ledru-Rollin) are lined with home decoration boutiques, record and designer label stores. Along the **rue du Faubourg-Saint-Antoine** (Bastille, Ledru-Rollin) you'll find furniture and clothes stores.

Les Fleurs – *6 passage Josset - Ledru-Rollin - closed Sun.* This store is packed with jewellery, handbags, stationary, mugs and decorative objects.

La Bellevilloise

Sensitive et Fils – *31 r. Faidherbe - Faidherbe-Chaligny - closed Sun.* An Asian inspired store that sells fabric, furniture, colourful clothes and enamelled plates.

NIGHTLIFE

The bars along the **rues de Lappe, de la Roquette** and **de Charonne**, which lie between the Bastille and Ledru-Rollin, are jampacked at weekends. The **rues Oberkampf et Jean-Pierre Timbaud** (Oberkampf, Parmentier), in the north of 11th arr., are also favorites with night-time revellers.

Badaboum – *2 bis r. des Taillandiers - Ledru-Rollin.* This fashionable address combines a cosy cocktail bar and a club playing house and electro music.

Joséphine - Caves Parisiennes – *25 r. Moret - Ménilmontant - closed Sun-Mon.* An elegant Art Déco bar that serves cocktails, rare whiskies, wine and snacks, while DJs add to the ambience.

L'International – *5-7 r. Moret - Ménilmontant - closed Sun.* A music venue for up-and-coming bands.

La Maroquinerie – *23 r. Boyer - Gambetta - www.lamaroquinerie.fr. Thisbar.* This bar-restaurant is also a well-known 500-seat concert venue with a pleasant terrace.

This eastern Paris district, with its mixed population, patchwork architecture, communal gardens, artists studios, mechanics workshops, and overgrown courtyards, is less touristy, but has a lively nightlife.

VISIT

Place de la Bastille – ⓜ Bastille. Nothing remains of the prison that once stood here, which was mobbed by revolutionaries on 14 July 1789. Today, this is the destination for protests and parades. In the center stands the **colonne de Juillet** which was erected in memory of the Parisians killed during the 1830 and 1848 Revolutions.

Opéra Bastille★ – ⓜ Bastille - www.operadeparis.fr - guided tours of public areas and backstage (€15) : for further information tel ℘ 01 40 01 19 70. The opera house, opened its doors in 1989. All types of craftsmen, from wigmakers to electricians, were hired to accomplish this opera. All the sets are designed and stored here. The ultramodern hall holds up to 2 700 spectators.

Cimetière du Père-Lachaise★★ – 16 r. du Repos - ⓜ Père-Lachaise. Take a romantic, and unusual, stroll through Paris's largest cemetery. Famous personalities lie under the trees: Chopin, Champollion, Beaumarchais, Oscar Wilde, Proust, Delacroix, Édith Piaf, and Jim Morrison.

WHERE TO EAT

🔟 Bistrot Paul Bert – 18 r. Paul-Bert - ⓜ Charonne - ℘ 01 43 72 24 01 - closed Sun-Mon - menus €18 (lunch), €41 (dinner) - reservations obligatory. A pleasant bistrot where home cooking takes pride of place. Expect to find rib steak, or ox cheek pie on the menu. Be sure to save room for the baba au rhum.

Cimetière du Père-Lachaise

🔢 Café de l'Industrie – 16 r. St-Sabin - ⓜ Bréguet-Sabin - ℘ 01 47 00 13 53 - http://cafedelindustrieparis.fr - main courses €11-19. Quality cuisine on offer in this typical, neighborhood bistrot.

🔢 Le Chardenoux – 1 r. Jules-Vallès - ⓜ Charonne - ℘ 01 43 71 49 52 - www.restaurantlechardenoux.com - closed Sun and Mon - breakfast menu (weekdays) €22, lunch €27, dinner €41. The charming bistrot by Cyril Lignac puts the tradition in the tradition: pâté en croûte, eggs en cocotte with porcini mushrooms, marinated salmon, duck hachis parmentier (like Sheperd's Pie), and plenty of desserts.

🔢 Le Sot l'y laisse – 70 r. Alexandre-Dumas - ⓜ Alexandre-Dumas - ℘ 01 40 09 79 20 - closed Sat and Mon lunch and all day Sun - lunch menu €19-25, main courses €25. Originating from Osaka, chef Eiji Doihara, pays homage to French gastronomy at this lovely bistrot, which has a well-earned reputation.

🔢 Le Temps au Temps – 13 r. Paul-Bert - ⓜ Charonne - ℘ 01 43 79 63 40 - closed Sun-Mon - menus €20-22 (lunch), €28-32 (dinner). Delicious bistrot-style dishes make up the menu, the chalked-up choices include: potted meat, and mackerel open sandwich, rack of veal and eggplant caviar, baba au rhum and peaches in syrup.

🔢 Mélac – 42 r. Léon-Frot - ⓜ Charonne - ℘ 01 43 70 59 27 - closed Sun-Mon -lunch menu €15, main courses €15-25. Savour authentic Aveyrnon dishes at this charming bistrot.

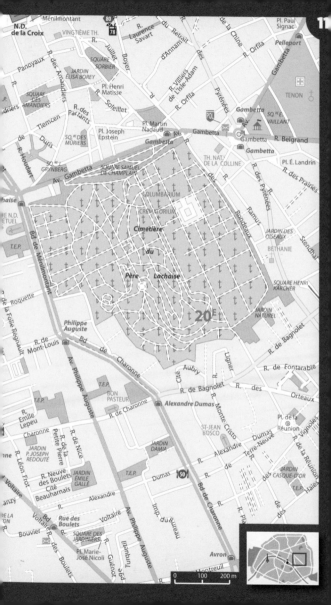

📍29 À La Biche au Bois – *45 av. Ledru-Rollin - ⊜ Gare-de-Lyon - ℘ 01 43 43 34 38 - closed Mon lunch, Sat lunch and Sun - main courses €17-25.* A lively spot to enjoy big plates of traditional cuisine, including seasonal game. Excellent service.

📍22 Coco de Mer – *34 bd St-Marcel - ⊜ St-Marcel - ℘ 01 47 07 06 64 - www.cocodemer.fr - closed Sun and Mon - main courses €12-20.* Imagine you're in the Seychelles, with a glass of punch in hands and your feet in the sand. The menu here, heavy on seafood, will transport you.

📍57 L'Auberge Aveyronnaise – *40 r. Gabriel-Lamé - ⊜ Cour-St-Émilion - ℘ 01 43 40 12 24 - menus from €20.* Checkered tablecloths add a rustic feel to this restaurant that specializes in Aveyron cuisine.

📍41 Le Baron Rouge – *1 r. Théophile-Roussel - ⊜ Ledru-Rollin - closed Mon lunch, Sun eve - platters around €10.* This neighbourhood hub is the perfect place to enjoy good wine, accompanied by a platter of cheese or charcuterie.

📍45 Le Cotte Rôti – *1 r. de Cotte - ⊜ Ledru-Rollin - ℘ 01 43 45 06 37 - closed Sat lunch, Sun and Mon - menus €22 (lunch), €39 (dinner).* A modern bistrot that serves a market-driven menu.

📍53 Le Temps des Cerises – *18 r. de la Butte-aux-Cailles - ⊜ Place-d'Italie - ℘ 01 45 89 69 48 - www.letemps descerisescoop.com - closed Sun - menus €13.50 (lunch), €21-25 (dinner).* A bistrot that is emblematic in the Butte, that prepares unpretentious bistrot dishes.

TAKE A BREAK

📍7 Carl Marletti – *51 r. Censier - ⊜ Censier- Daubenton - closed Sun-Mon eve.* Their homemade cakes are delicious. Choose a classic (*millefeuille, baba au rhum*) or go for the gorgeous éclairs in a riot of colours.

📍17 La Mosquée de Paris – *39 r. Geoffroy-St-Hilaire - ⊜ Censier-Daubenton.* This is a great spot to relax and sip a mint tea, whilst nibbling an oriental pastry.

SHOPPING

📍68 Marché et brocante d'Aligre – *Pl. d'Aligre - ⊜ Ledru-Rollin - Tue-Sun 7h-14h.* This bustling market, popular with locals, doubles as a flea market.

📍73 Sabah – *77 r. Crozatier - ⊜ Ledru-Rollin.* This grocery store stocks a treasure trove of of oriental goods - a real Ali Baba's cave.

NIGHTLIFE

⊕ The many bars clustered along the **rue Mouffetard** are still popular with students.

📍98 Le China – *50 r. de Charenton - ⊜ Ledru-Rollin.* The 1930s Shanghai décor and the delicious cocktails are two good reasons to try this bar.

📍83 Le Batofar – *Face au 11 quai F.-Mauriac - ⊜ Bibliothèque-F.-Mitterrand - www.batofar.org.* A Paris barge hosting a variety of events: concerts, night-club, terrace restaurant and even a beach during summer months

📍88 Le Petit Bain – *7 port de la Gare - ⊜ Bibliothèque-F.-Mitterrand - www.petit bain.org - closed Mon.* A bright yellow barge with a restaurant, live music, friendly bar and lovely sundeck.

Le Batofar

Breathe in a gulp of learned air at theJardin des Plantes, drink tea at the Mosquée de Paris, saunter through the villages of Mouffetard and the Butte-aux-Cailles, admire the modern architecture of the BNF and Bercy... With such a wealth of things to do and see, you'll be spoilt for choice!

Muséum national d'Histoire naturelle

VISIT

Jardin des Plantes★★ –
Pl. Valhubert - 🚇 *Gare-d'Austerlitz.*
Escape the urban bustle in these attractive gardens. Take a stroll around the greenhouses, the alpine garden and the **ménagerie**★, one of the oldest zoos (1794) still active *(9h-18h, winter 17h - €13).*

Muséum national d'Histoire naturelle★★ – 🚇 *Gare-d'Austerlitz - www.mnhn.fr - 10h-18h - closed Tue - €9.*
For 400 years this splendid museum has been devoted to nature and its relationship with man. Without a doubt, the **Grande Galerie de l'Évolution**★★★ with its 7000 specimens is the highlight of the visit.

Grande Mosquée de Paris★ –
🚇 *Censier-Daubenton - 9h-12h, 14h-18h - closed Fri - €3.* This beautiful building, with its Hispanic-Mauresque architecture, was built in memory of muslim soldiers killed in First World War. This oasis of calm also proposes a hammam, a restaurant and a tearoom (☕ *Take a Break*).

Quartier Mouffetard★ – 🚇 *Place-Monge.* Worth a visit is the **place de la Contrescarpe** with its café terraces, and the **rue Mouffetard** which is lined with small shops and lively bars.

La Butte-aux-Cailles★ – 🚇 *Place-d'Italie.* A village-like charm prevails in this district, with its labyrinth of cobbled streets and small houses. The wine bar and bistrots still have a working class atmosphere.

Bibliothèque nationale de France - site François Mitterrand★ – 🚇 *Bibliothèque-F.-Mitterrand - 10h-20h, Sun 13h-19h - closed Mon.* Designed by Dominique Perrault, the library building has four 80m high towers representing open books.

Parc de Bercy★ – 🚇 *Bercy.* The wooded 14-hectare park stretches from the **Bercy Arena** – which hosts sports events and concerts – and the cour Saint-Émilion.

Cour Saint-Émilion – 🚇 *Cour-St-Émilion.* The ancient warehouses, lined up along a pretty cobbled street, now house leisure and home goods stores, bistrots and restaurants.

Musée des Arts Forains★ – *Hors plan - 53 av. des Terroirs-de-France -* 🚇 *Cour-St-Émilion - www.arts-forains.com - 26 Dec through 7 Jan - €14 (rest of year by reservation only).* This magical place stirs childhood memories, with carousels, automata and barrel organs.

Viaduc des Arts - Promenade plantée★ – 🚇 *Gare-de-Lyon.* The arches of the viaduc des Arts, which borders the avenue Dausmenil, are home to stores and craft workshops. Along the top, the former railway line has been converted into a pleasant pedestrian pathway.

WHERE TO EAT

☺ Best to avoid the pseudo-rustic restaurants along the rue Mouffetard.

from town halls and the tourist office.

Vélib' – ☏ 01 30 79 79 30 - www.velib.paris. Buy a one-day (€1.70), or 7-day ticket (8 €). The first half-hour is free; the second half-hour costs €1. From the 3rd half-hour: €4 per half-hour. There is a €150 deposit.

Paris à Vélo C'est Sympa! – www.parisvelosympa.com - €12 for 1/2 day, €15/1 day, €20/24h, €25/2 days. - deposit €250 - guided tours: €35.

Bike'n Roller – ☏ 01 45 50 38 27 - bikehire : €12 1/2 day, €17/1 day - a deposit is required.

Taxi

When the taxi sign is green the taxi is available, when the sign is red it is busy. You can hail down a cab in the street. There is a basic starting charge which is added onto the price of the journey.

Taxis bleus – ☏ 36 09 (0.15 €/mn) - www.taxis-bleus.com.

Taxis G7 – ☏ 36 07 (0.15 €/mn) - www.taxisG7.fr. Credit cards are accepted for over €15.

Ridesharing

Ridesharing apps **Le Taxi**, **Zaleou**, **Tafixy**, and **Uber** can all be used in Paris.

MONEY AND BUDGET

Banks – You can find ATMs all over Paris. Banks are usually open Monday to Friday from 9h to 17h30, some open on Saturday mornings from 9h to 12h. Credit cards are widely accepted.

Budget – Paris is a bit less costly than London or New York. Expect to pay about €100-150 per night in a decent hotel, €20-25 for a meal in a basic restaurant, €35-50 for a meal in a good restaurant, €8.50-12 for an entrance ticket to museum, €4-6 for a glass of wine, and €8-12 for a cocktail (during happy hour).

DISCOUNTS AND PASSES

Paris Museum Pass – www.parismuseumpass.com - 2-day/€48, 4-day/€62, 6-day/€74. This pass offers unlimited priority (no queuing) admission to more than 60 museums (permanent collections) and monuments in and around Paris. You can buy it online, or at museums, tobacconists and the Paris tourist office. 🚸 it isn't worth buying if you are under 26: you qualify for free entry to a large number of sites. *(see opposite)*.

Paris-Visite – www.ratp.fr - zones 1-3: €13.20/1 day; €21.50/2 day; €2.40/3 day and €42.20/5 day (discount for kids 11 and under). This pass gives you unlimited travel on the metro, bus, tram, RER and Transilien for 1, 2, 3 or 5 days, and reductions to some sites and activities (consult the list on www.ratp.fr).

Paris Passlib' – www.parisinfo.com - 2-day/ €109, 3-day/ €129, 5-day/

GETTING AROUND PARIS

RATP – ✆ 32 46 (€0.34/mn) - www.ratp.fr. **www.vianavigo.com** – A website that provides information on routes and timetables for public transport, in and around Paris.

Metro

The quickest way to get around the capital. There are 14 metro lines in Paris. Avoid travelling in rush hour (8h-9h30, 17h-18h30). It takes about 2min per station and 5min to change.

Hours – From 5h30 to midnight/1h (Fri.-Sat. and the eve of a public holiday: 2h).

Bus

Network – There are 159 lines which complement the subway system.

Noctilien Bus – There are 47 night bus routes (0h30-5h30). They depart from the stations at Gare-de-Lyon, Gare-de-l'Est, Gare-St-Lazare, Gare-Montparnasse and Châtelet. Two circular lines, N 01 (interior) and N 02 (exterior) link popular Paris nightspots.

RER

Network – The RER has 5 lines, 3 depart from Châtelet-Les-Halles (lines A, B and D). The RER is the best option for travelling to the Paris suburbs (Versailles, Disneyland, Roissy and Orly airports), but less practical for Paris *intra-muros* trips since the stops are further apart.

Tramway

Relevant Lines – Lines T3a and T3b run along boulevards des Maréchaux, from Pont du Garigliano (15th arr.) to Porte de la Chapelle (1 8th arr.), connecting with bus, metro and RER .

Tickets

Ticket t+ – This ticket is valid for the **metro** and **RER** (Paris *intra-muros* only), ticket t+ allows you to ride the entire network with unlimited transfers.

On the **bus**, a ticket t+ is valid for travel along the entire line (except for lines 299, 350 and 351) and allows transfers from bus/bus, bus/tram and tram/tram. It remains valid for any transfers within 90 minutes. However, for any RER journey **outside Paris** the same ticket is not valid, and the cost depends on distance.

Tickets – Tickets are sold at metro and RER stations, on the bus and at tobacconists. They can be purchased individually, or packs of ten (carnet).

Tarifs – Ticket t+: €1.90; pack of 10 tickets: €14.50.

Ⓢ Subscriptions : ♿ *Discounts and passes* (**Paris-Visite** pass).

Batobus

✆ 0 825 05 01 01 - www.batobus.com. Taking a river bus along the Seine river is an original, but expensive, way to explore the main quartiers and monuments in Paris. (♿ *Visits and activities*).

Stop-off points – Tour Eiffel, Musée d'Orsay, St-Germain-des-Prés, Notre-Dame, Jardin des Plantes, Hôtel de Ville, Louvre and Champs-Élysées.

Times – 10h-21h30, every 20min (19h low season, every 25min).

Ticket prices – A one-day pass (€17), 2 -day (€19) or yearly (€60).

Bike

There are 220 km of cycle paths in Paris. The *Paris à vélo* plan is available

WHEN TO GO

Seasons

Paris pulls in tourists all year long. However, the influx of tourists peaks at **Christmas, New Year, Easter** and **summer**, and during the dates of the major professional salons and fairs. During these periods it is advisable to reserve your stay well in advance.

Calendar of Events

Chinese New Year – *Late Jan or early Feb.* Parades in the 13th arr. and the Belleville quartier.

Paris Marathon – *Early Apr.* From the Champs-Élysées to the avenue Foch.

Nuit des Musées – *May.* Different Paris museums host events.

Gay Pride – *Jun.* A parade through the streets of Paris.

Fête foraine des Tuileries – *Jun-Aug.* Fairground in the Jardin des Tuileries.

Paris Jazz Festival – *From mid-Jun to Jul.* Open-air concerts *(w.-end)*, in the Parc floral de Paris (Vincennes).

Paris Plage – *From Jul to mid-Aug.* Beaches and activities on the banks of the Seine.

Open-air cinema – *From Jul to mid-Aug.* Free films in the Parc de La Villette.

Bastille Day, 14 July – Proms, fireworks and military parade.

Heritage Days – *3rd w.-end Sept.* Monuments that are usually closed to the public open their doors.

Nuit Blanche – *Oct.* Artistic installations and performances in the city.

Fête des vendanges – *2nd w.-end Oct.* Takes place at the Butte Montmartre.

Fiac – *Late Oct.* international Contemporary Art Fair at the Grand Palais, Louvre and city outskirts

Open-air skating rinks – *Dec-Feb.* In front of the Hôtel-de-Ville, Montparnasse station and BNF.

⊛ For further information consult the tourist office website : www.parisinfo.com

Paris Plage

GETTING TO PARIS

By train

☎ 36 35 (0.34 €/mn) - www.voyages-sncf.com. Trains from the Southeast of France, arrive at the **Gare de Lyon** (12th arr.). From the Center: **Gare d'Austerlitz** (13th arr.). From Brittany and Southwest : **Gare Montparnasse** (15th arr.). From the North: **Gare du Nord** (10th arr.). From the North and East: **Gare de l'Est** (10tharr.). From Normandy: **Gare St-Lazare** (9tharr.). **Eurostar** runs from London (St Pancras) to Gare du Nord in under 3hrs www.eurostar.com.

By plane

Charles-de-Gaulle Airport – www.parisaeroport.fr - 23 km north of Paris. To reach Paris, take **RER B** direction St-Rémy-lès-Chevreuse-Massy (30min to city centre, €10.30). By **bus**, Direct Bus (1h15, €17) or Roissybus (1h, €13.20). **Taxi** price is fixed: €50 (Right Bank), €55 (Left Bank). **Orly Airport** – www.paris aeroport.fr - 11 km south of Paris. To reach Paris, take **Orlyval** to Antony then **RER** line B direction Mitry-Claye/CDG airport (35min, €12.10). By **bus**: Bus Direct (35min, €12) or Orlybus (30min, €9.20). **Taxi** price is fixed: €35 (Right Bank) €30 (Left Bank). **Paris-Beauvais Airport** - www.aeroportbeauvais.com - 80 km north of Paris. Shuttle buses run from Porte Maillot, Paris (1h15, €15.90).

ENTERTAINMENT

Paris has a long-standing reputation of being a hub of entertainment. There is a wealth of theatres, legendary cabarets, trendy clubs and mythical concert halls.

Program – Consult the listings of events which are published in: *L'Officiel des spectacles*, *Pariscope* and *Télérama's* weekly supplement *Sortir*. Useful websites include: www.sortiraparis.com; www.timeout.com/paris; http://quefaire.paris.fr; www.evene.lefigaro.fr; www.lebonbon.fr/paris; www.parisbouge.com. The websites www.parisnightlife.fr and http://parislanuit.fr produce lists, on a day-to-day basis, of night-time shows and diverse entertainment.

Reservation and discounts – www.billetreduc.com; www.ticketac.com; www.theatreonline.com (last-minute tickets). Also see Kiosques Théâtre and Jeunes (♿ *Discounts and passes*).

MAIL/POST

Bureau de poste du Louvre – 52 r. du Louvre - ⓜ Sentier, Bourse - open daily and non-stop 24h/24.

WHERE TO STAY

Paris is made up of a diversity of quartiers each with its own particular ambiance. Some are residential (7th, 15th, 16th arr.), others have a reputation for their nightlife (3rd, 10th, 11th arr.), for being chic (6th, 7th,

Tourist Information

Online:
www.parisinfo.com
(Paris Tourist Office)
www.paris.fr
(City of Paris website)

In Paris:
Tourist Office visitors' centre – 25 r. des Pyramides - ⓜ Pyramides - June-Oct : 9h-19h; Nov-May : 10h-19h.

8th arr.), or family orientated (12th, 13th, 14th, 15th arr.). The choice is yours. Below is a list of general and specialist websites to help you with accommodation in Paris. You will find something to suit your taste and your budget.

Hotels – There is a selection of hotels on www.hotelaparis.com, www.viamichelin.com or www.booking.com.

Bed and breakfast – Consult the websites www.chambre-ville.com; www.goodmorningparis.fr; www.authenticbandbparis.com.

Youth Hostels – Fédération unie des auberges de jeunesse (www.fuaj.org); Ligue Française des Auberges de Jeunesse (www.auberges-de-jeunesse.com). Some of the most modern hostels are Les Piaules (11th arr. - www.lespiaules.com), Generator Hostel (10th arr. - http://generatorhostels.com), St Christopher's Inn (10th and 19th arr. - www.st-christophers.co.uk).

Appartment rental – This a good option if you are staying for longer than a weekend. Reservations can be made on www.we-paris.com; www.apartments-and-more-paris.com; www.apartmentparis.fr; www.homelidays.com ; www.airbnb.com. ♿ Another useful website to consult is **www.parisinfo.com**

© Sébastien Rabany / Photononstop

ardens and parks – These open
between 8h and 9h30 ; the closing
times vary according to the season.

Public holidays – 1st January, Easter
Monday, 1st and 8th May, Ascension
Thursday, Whit Monday, 14th July,
15th August, 1st and 11th November,
25th December. Most museums and
monuments are closed for 1st January,
May and 25th December (check for
other public holidays).

HERE TO EAT

aurants – The choices are
less. Over recent years, a
movement has emerged the
nomie, a refined and creative
sion of bistrot dishes. There are a
ge number of restaurants serving
every type of international cuisine..

Most restaurants serve from 12h to
14h, and 19h/20h to 22h. Generally
brasseries serve food all day long.

Specialities – In classic bistrots the
menu usually features egg mayon-
naise (similar to deviled eggs) or
homemade terrine as starters, beef
tartare or fish dish of the day for the
main, and crème brûlée or tarte tatin
for dessert.

WHAT TO DO AND SEE

Bateaux-mouches – A must-do for
any visitor to Paris! Choose from:
www.bateauxparisiens.com, www.
vedettesdeparis.com, www.paris
canal.com, www.canauxrama.com.
Pay about €15 for a 1h cruise, and
€80-100 for a dinner cruise.

Tourist buses – There are
guided tours of the city with:
www. carsrouges.com,
www.pariscityrama.com,
www.paris.opentour. com.

Paris insolite – There are unusual
ways to explore Paris. Take a tour of
the **catacombes** (www.catacombes.
paris.fr - daily, except Mon 10h-
20h30 - €13) or the capital's **sewers**

(www.paris.fr - 11h-18h, winter 17h
- closed Thu-Fri - €4.40). Discover
Paris in a **2CV** (www.4roues-sous-
1parapluie.com) or **rickshaw** (www.
paris-tuktuk.fr).

Take an **urban walk** in 18th, 19th and
20th arr. with Ça se visite (✆ 01 43 57
59 50 - www.ca-se-visite.fr - €12).

Editorial Director: Cynthia Ochterbeck
Editorial: Sophie Friedman
Contributing Writers: Nick Taylor, Lyn Parry, Anna
Crine, Matilde Miñon-Marqua, María Guttiérez-
Alonso, Guylaine Idoux, Hervé Kerros, Sarah
Larrue, Sarah Parot, Pierre Plantier
Cartography: Laurence Sénéchal, Daniel Duguay,
Alain Robert
Cover & Interior Design: Laurent Muller
Additional Layout: Natasha George
Photo research: Yoshimi Kanazawa,
Marie Simonet, Maria Gaspar

Special Sales: travel.lifestyle@us.michelin.com
Contact us: Michelin Travel & Lifestyle North
America, One Parkway South, Greenville,
SC 29615, USA
travel.lifestyle@us.michelin.com

Michelin Travel Partner, Hannay House,
39 Clarendon Road, Watford, Herts WD17 1JA, UK
travelpubsales@uk.michelin.com
www.ViaMichelin.com

Printed: February 2018

While every effort is made to ensure that all
information printed in this guide is correct and
up-to-date, Michelin Travel Partner accepts no
liability for any direct, indirect or consequential
losses howsoever caused so far as such can be
excluded by law. Admission prices listed for
sights in this guide are for a single adult, unless
otherwise specified.

Mapping: © MICHELIN et © 2013-2014 TomTom.
All rights reserved. This material is proprietary
and the subject of copyright protection, database
right protection and other intellectual property
rights owned by TomTom or its suppliers.
The use of this material is subject to the terms of
a license agreement. Any unauthorized copying
or disclosure of this material will lead to criminal
and civil liabilities.

€155 (discount for youth, kids). This package, the official Paris tourist office pass, includes the Paris-Visite Pass Zones 1-3, the Paris Museum Pass, a trip on a bateau-mouche and an open-top bus tour. This pass can be purchased at the tourist office, or online at www.parisinfo.com.

Free entry – All European Union Citizens under 26 (ID is required) get free entry to the majority of state museums and monuments. For those over 26, state museums are free 1st Sunday of each month. Entrance to the permanent collections in Ville de Paris museums, except for Notre Dame's acheological crypt, is free for everybody.

Parisien d'un jour – www.greeters. paris. These Parisian volunteers propose free walking tours, on request, for groups of 1 to 6 people. They take visitors off the beaten tourist path to discover the other side of Paris.

Kiosques Théâtre – Theater tickets are sold at half price (for the best seats), for same-day performances. Pl. de la Madeleine (⋒ Madeleine); parvis de la gare Montparnasse (⋒ Montparnasse-Bienvenüe); place des Ternes (⋒ Ternes). Info: www. kiosqueculture.com

Kiosques Jeunes – For the under 29s, free invitations, and reduced-price tickets are on offer for cultural events such as concerts, shows and plays. Location: Canopée (10, passage de la Canopée - ⋒ Châtelet - Tue-Sat 11h-19h); Champ-de-Mars (101 quai Branly - ⋒ Bir-Hakeim - Tue-Fri

13h-18h); Goutte-d'Or (centre musical Barbara - 1 r. Fleury - ⋒ Barbès-Rochechouart - Tue-Fri 11h-19h).

OPENING HOURS AND PUBLIC HOLIDAYS

Shops – Generally open 10h-19h, closed Sun. Independent food shops are often open Sunday mornings but closed Mondays. Many grocery stores stay open until late evening.

Department stores – 10h-19h, and tend to stay open late once a week until 21h30/22h.

Bars and cafés – They often open early (7h or 8h) and close around 2h. 🍹 Drinks are cheaper during **Happy hour**, usually from 17h/18h to 20h.

Museums and monuments – The ticket offices normally shut half an hour before the building's closing time. They also close every Monday or Tuesday.

The **illuminations** of briges and monuments are switched on at dusk. The best way to enjoy this spectacle is to take a river boat cruise (**🕒 What to see and do**). The Eiffel tower sparkles 5min every hour.

Churches – You may not visit while a church service is taking place. They generally close between 12h and 14h.

Sundays in Paris

A lot of stores stay open on Sundays in Paris. This is the case in the Marais (🕒 *Quartier 4*), on the Champs-Élysées (🕒 *Quartier 7*) or at the Carrousel du Louvre (🕒 *Quartier 2*). The quays along the banks of the Saint-Martin canal are exclusively reserved for pedestrians on Sundays, from the rue de Lancry to Jaurès (🕒 *Quartier 10*). here as well, many stores stay open. Go ahead and treat yourself to a leisurely brunch at a tea room, or local bistrot.

INDEX

MICHELIN

Michelin Travel Partner

Société par actions simplifiées au capital de 11 288 880 EUR
27 cours de l'Île Seguin - 92100 Boulogne Billancourt (France)
R.C.S. Nanterre 433 677 721

No part of this publication may be reproduced in any form
without the prior permission of the publisher.

© Michelin Travel Partner
Printer: SOLER (Spain)
Printed in Spain: 2-2018 ISO 14001